CONSERVATISM

FROM JOHN ADAMS TO CHURCHILL

BOOKS BY PETER VIERECK

I. Poetry:

Terror and Decorus. Charles Scribner's Sons, New York, 1948. Pulitzer Prize, 1949.
Strike Through the Mask! Scribner's, 1950.
The First Morning. Scribner's, 1952.
The Persimmon Tree. Scribner's, 1956.

II. Prose:

Metapolitics: From the Romantics to Hitler. Alfred A. Knopf, New York. Out of print. (Swedish edition, 1942; Italian edition, 1948.)
Conservatism Revisited: The Revolt Against Revolt. Scribner's, 1949. Out of print. (British edition, 1950.)
Shame and Glory of the Intellectuals: Babbitt Jr. vs. the Rediscovery of Values. The Beacon Press, Boston, 1953. Out of print.
Dream and Responsibility: Four Test Cases of the Tension Between Poetry and Society. The University Press of Washington, D.C., 1953.
The Unadjusted Man. Beacon Press, Boston, 1956. Reprinted as Capricorn paperback, G. Putnam Sons, New York, 1962.
Conservatism: From John Adams to Churchill. Anvil paperback, Van Nostrand Co., Princeton, New Jersey, 1956. (Japanese edition, 1957 by Japan Institute of Foreign Affairs; Spanish edition in Buenos Aires, 1959; Korean edition, 1960.)
Metapolitics: The Roots of the Nazi Mind. Capricorn pocketbook, G. P. Putnam's Sons, New York, 1961.
Conservatism Revisited and *The New Conservatism: What Went Wrong?,* two books in one (book I a reprint, book II new), Collier Books, New York, 1962.

III. Verse Drama:

The Tree Witch. Scribner's, New York, 1961.

CONSERVATISM

FROM JOHN ADAMS TO CHURCHILL

PETER VIERECK

Professor of History
Mount Holyoke College

AN ANVIL ORIGINAL

under the general editorship of

LOUIS L. SNYDER

D. VAN NOSTRAND COMPANY, INC.

PRINCETON, NEW JERSEY

TORONTO   LONDON

NEW YORK

To the memory and tradition of

WINSTON CHURCHILL

"The principal instrument of America is freedom; of Russia, slavery."—Alexis de Tocqueville

"Society cannot exist unless a controlling power upon will and appetite be placed somewhere; and the less of it there is within, the more of it there must be without."—Edmund Burke

"Back out of all this now too much for us . . .
Here are your waters and your watering place.
Drink and be whole again beyond confusion."
Robert Frost

D. VAN NOSTRAND COMPANY, INC.
120 Alexander St., Princeton, New Jersey (*Principal office*); 24 West 40 St., New York, N.Y.
D. VAN NOSTRAND COMPANY (Canada), LTD.
25 Hollinger Rd., Toronto 16, Canada
D. VAN NOSTRAND COMPANY, LTD.
358, Kensington High Street, London, W.14, England

PREFACE

This brief new history of conservatism is planned for two audiences: the serious general reader and the college community.[1] There have been excellent lengthier works, often intended for partisans or for specialists, but none aiming to meet the need for a concise, balanced picture and for an anthology (Part II of this book) of the chief conservative writers.

Across America, conservatism is being hotly debated without definition or historical context. The first chapter defines conservatism itself; the second, its special technical terms; the third describes its changing historical context; the rest deal with its actual thinkers and statesmen. After each main conservative thesis, the anti-conservative rebuttal is summarized (cf. page 17), and the reader is allowed to reach his own conclusions. Though the first stress is on conservative political philosophy (from John Adams to Churchill), key sections also stress non-political conservatism: in religion (Cardinal Newman) and in the primarily cultural protest against material progress (Coleridge, Dostoyevsky, Melville, Henry Adams).

Every major point made in Part I, the narrative section, is concretely illustrated by an appended cross-reference to a primary source in Part II, the document anthology. Some of the challenging foreign documents are not elsewhere available in English, either because they are out of print (Maistre, Cortés, Barrès, Pobiedonostsev), untranslated (Gentz, Burckhardt), or unsatisfactorily translated (Nietzsche). Accordingly the author has made his own translations where necessary, as noted in footnotes.

[1] In the special case of the college audience, the range of contents over Europe, England, America, from 1770 through today, may perhaps prove serviceable in some instances for courses in that same range of countries, dates, or fields: intellectual history; American history; European history; British history; political science; government; social psychology; general education.

Criteria for inclusion were three: representativeness, depth of perception, importance of influence. The result is not uniformity but a gamut: from extreme intolerant reaction to an evolutionary moderate spirit. The former passes imperceptibly into authoritarianism; the latter, into liberalism. Some readers may quite reasonably prefer to classify the borderline cases not as "conservatives" but as "authoritarians" at the one border and "liberals" at the other. The present classification, however, assumes that no "pure" conservatives ever exist; all are diluted in varying degrees with either authoritarianism or liberalism—Maistre and Burke being the respective prototypes of these two dilutions. In organizing this considerable material with maximum conciseness, the aim is limited, unpretending: no new trail of truth, beauty, or polity but rather clarity, sobriety, impersonality, documentation. To clarify is not the same as to oversimplify. Conservatism is hardly simple, being more an implicit temperament, less an articulate philosophy than the other famous isms.

PETER VIERECK

The author acknowledges with particular gratitude the generous technical and intellectual help of Mrs. Frances Head in preparing the manuscript for the printer.

TABLE OF CONTENTS

PART I

CONSERVATISM

I GENERAL

— 1 —

HISTORICAL AND PHILOSOPHICAL ORIGINS OF CONSERVATISM

Begins with Burke. The birth of a deliberate international conservatism is dated by Edmund Burke's essay of 1790, *Reflections on the Revolution in France,* in the same way that the birth of international Marxism is dated by the *Communist Manifesto* of 1848. Lord Hugh Cecil, a leading twentieth-century philosopher of conservatism, defined that ism as "a force called into activity by the French Revolution [*of 1789*] and operating against the tendencies that that Revolution set up." Those who consider this definition too narrow will, in addition, stress the many broader implications of the Latin verb from which it is derived: *conservare,* meaning "to preserve."

Burke himself did not use the noun "conservatism," although he did use the verb "to conserve." Wide usage of the noun first began among European traditionalists of the early nineteenth century, groping for a new philosophical terminology to use against the French Revolutionary era of 1789-1815, especially against its most radical and terrorist party, the Jacobins. Proponents associated that era with its appealing democratic slogan, "Liberty, Equality, Fraternity," and with its liberation of the masses from feudal exploiters. Opponents associated the era with the murder of innocent victims by the Jacobins during 1793-1794 and with the aggressions of Napoleon during 1799-1815. Proponents of the era believed that its idealistic ends, its democratic social gains, outweighed the bad means used and the millions of Europeans killed in that quarter-century of wars. Oppo-

nents believed that the bad means outweighed the democratic, liberal, and rationalist ends. The more tradition-
bound opponents also questioned the ends themselves.
After 1815, these ends suffered—according to proponents,
suffered undeservedly—from the general revulsion against
the means. That revulsion gave conservatives their first
great opportunity for restoring the pre-revolutionary traditions; a sudden flowering of more than one brand of
conservative philosophy followed.

Rival Brands of Conservative. It would unfairly
stack the cards in favor of conservatism to present only
the moderate brand, founded by Burke (1729-1797), and
to omit the more extreme brand, founded by Joseph de
Maistre (1753-1821). The former is evolutionary; the
latter, counter-revolutionary. Both favor tradition against
the innovations of 1789, but their traditions differ: the
former fights against 1789 for the sake of traditional
liberties; the latter, for the sake of traditional *authority.*
The former is not authoritarian but constitutionalist, often
parliamentary. The latter is partly authoritarian, in its
stress on the authority of some traditional élite, and is
often called not "conservative" but "reactionary." However, to call it "totalitarian" would go much too far.
Its authority does not try to be "total," in the sense of taking over the total personality, the total culture, but is
restricted to politics (and sometimes also religion). That
distinction between authoritarian and totalitarian separates even the most reactionary conservative from the
totalitarian fascists, nazis, and communists. So does the
distinction between monarchist authority, normally
checked by the leash of tradition, and the untraditional,
hence unchecked despotism of the upstart plebeian dictators of totalitarianism.

Terminology: Reactionary "Ottantottist" vs. Evolutionary "Burkean." A reactionary king of Piedmont-
Sardinia became almost a figure of fun by wandering
about mumbling pathetically the word "ottantott'," Italian
for '88. Thereby he meant to say: all problems would
vanish if only the world turned its clock back to 1788,
the year before the Revolution. We may accordingly coin
the adjective "ottantottist" for the counter-revolutionary
and authoritarian conservative, the adjective "Burkean"
for the evolutionary and constitutional conservative. The
ottantottist sometimes seems just as revolutionary against

the existing present as the radical Jacobin or the Marxist, only in the opposite direction. The Burkean, in contrast, does come to terms with the reality of inevitable change. But he does so without the liberal's optimism and faith in progress.

Examples of Burkeans are John Adams in America, Tocqueville in France, Churchill in England. Examples of ottantottists are Maistre, Bonald, and Veuillot in France, Pobiedonostsev in Russia. But that distinction must not be oversimplified or overapplied. Human beings are complex, inconsistent; many conservatives do not fully lend themselves to neat pigeon-holing in either category but overlap—for example, Metternich in Austria and Calhoun in America. Each conservative listed briefly in this survey chapter receives longer analysis in subsequent chapters. Most are also represented in Part II: by primary-source documents, to be consulted side by side with the relevant discussions in Part I.

This division into Burke and Maistre wings does not mean both were equal in importance or influence. No work of Maistre on the French Revolution, no book by any ottantottist, has approached the influence of Burke's classic. Burke's arguments were borrowed, sometimes word for word, by all subsequent conservatives, including ottantottists. Maistre's conservatism, with its rigid monarchism, is today dying out. Burke's more flexible conservatism is today stronger than ever, permeating all parties in England and America. Burke, above all, was the *first* to formulate the conservative rebuttal to the French Revolution; all the others came later. Even among the non-Burkeans or reactionaries, Maistre is being supplanted in intellectual primacy by the Spanish philosopher, Donoso Cortés (1809-1853).

Radicals and Liberals on the French Revolution. What of those who did not have an attitude of *conservare* toward the traditional order and traditional values? They came to be called either liberals or radicals in the early nineteenth century, greatly differing from each other in degree and in methods. Their starting point, too, was in many cases the French Revolution. Liberals supported its early phase of rapid but peaceful change and were later frightened off; radicals sometimes defended even its later phases of violent change, terror, secret police, class war. Those who supported some or much of the French

Revolution and who hated Burke as its slanderer, often looked for guidance to Jean-Jacques Rousseau (1712-1778) in France and to Thomas Paine (1737-1809) in America and England. Both these influences on modern liberalism and radicalism tended to believe in two things: the natural goodness of man and the instinctive rightness of the masses. The conservative, whether Burkean or ottantottist, believes in neither.

Rousseau. Rousseau's *Emile,* 1762, has been called the fountainhead of modern liberal "progressive education." Its thesis was: "God makes all things good. . . ." His *Social Contract,* also 1762, applied the same thesis of natural goodness to politics: "Man is born free but is everywhere in chains." The supposed chains were tradition, the past, the status quo—all now to be brushed aside by what he called the collective "General Will" of the masses. This oversimplified version of his actually more complex philosophy was the greatest single influence on the ideology of Maximilien Robespierre (1758-1794), radical Jacobin dictator of the violent phase of the French Revolution. Lawful, moderate liberals like Thomas Jefferson (1743-1826) were also influenced by Rousseau in their anti-conservative view of human nature.

Paine vs. Burke. A disciple of Rousseau, Paine denounced Burke for attacking the French Revolution. Paine's essay, *The Rights of Man,* 1791-1792, might be called the rebuttal of a rebuttal; its optimistic arguments for faith in progress and in human nature rebutted Burke's pessimistic essay of 1790. You can test whether you are by impulse a liberal or a conservative by whether you instinctively side with Paine or Burke in their great debate. That difference of impulse goes deeper than politics, has little to do with what American party you happen to vote for. Since both impulses are equally basic to the mind of man, the eternal debate—of which the Burke and Paine essays are mere symbols—will never be permanently won by either side. It may be an unfairly personal argument to observe that when optimistic Tom Paine went to Paris to participate in his expected utopia, he was jailed by the very revolution he had defended against Burke's charge of terror.

Original Sin Necessitates Traditional Framework. Whether intentionally or unconsciously, whether literally or as a metaphor for behavior, conservatives apply to

politics the Christian doctrine of man's innate Original
Sin. Herein lies a key distinction between conservatives
and liberals. Men are not born naturally free or good
(assume conservatives) but naturally prone to anarchy,
evil, mutual destruction. What Rousseau calls the "chains"
that hinder man's goodness—society's traditional restrictions on the ego—are in reality the props that make
man good. They fit man into a stable, durable framework,
without which ethical behavior and responsible use of
liberty are impossible. (That framework may be monarchy, aristocracy, church, property, constitution, or
Supreme Court, depending on the country or era.) We
must peacefully alter that antiquated framework in accordance with more ideal blueprints, say moderate liberals
like Jefferson and John Stuart Mill. We must throw that
wicked framework overboard, say radicals and more
"advanced" liberals, descended from Rousseau or Paine.
No, we must preserve—*conservare*—that framework to
keep human nature ethical and free, say conservatives.

Private Property Defended. Anti-conservatives
sometimes attack private property. The French socialist
Proudhon defined "property" as "theft." Marxists define
it as the weapon of some exploiting class. Even many liberals deem property something about which to feel
slightly ashamed. Conservatives, however, take pride in
it. They argue that private property is a bulwark protecting not merely one class but all classes from chaos.
Anyone who gains hugely from property may, when criticized, invoke conservative arguments out of sheer self-
interest. Here lies the source of the bad name often given
to the word "conservative." A mere conservatism of the
pocketbook deserves that bad name; far from being a
bulwark against revolution, its irresponsibility often pro-
vokes revolution. More responsible conservatives, like
Disraeli or John Adams, defend property, their material
base, only when linked with a moral base: service to the
community. They distinguish sharply between a traditional, rooted property of service and a grasping, rootless
property, not yet mellowed by time. It is only the
loose journalistic use of "conservative," not the use by
serious philosophical conservatives like Burke, Maistre,
or Coleridge, that identifies conservatism with economic
commercialism or with the particular position held by
America's Old Guard Republicans.

Conservatives, Liberals Unite Against Totalitarianism. Another journalistic looseness identifies conservatism with softness toward fascism; liberalism, with softness toward communism. Only totalitarianism gains, in the opinion of moderates, when two such freedom-loving groups as liberals and conservatives question each other's good faith in opposing communism and fascism respectively. Conservatives and liberals will continue to differ about human nature, history, tradition, and the tempo of change. But to survive they find they must increasingly stand united against their common foe: totalitarianism, whether fascist or communist.

British Aspect. England is represented in greater length and detail than any other country in this book because so many authorities agree that hers is the most conservative temperament of all. Her conservative temperament is not a matter of any one political party or economic creed (in that narrow political sense her temperament is indeed liberal) but pervades the Labor party as much as the Conservative party. The result is to make her capitalists nondoctrinaire and her socialists gradualists. British conservatism, in the words of the Hapsburg Chancellor Metternich, "animates all classes" equally and thereby makes England "the freest land on earth *because* the most disciplined." During the Revolution of 1848, Tocqueville predicted that only "England is protected against the revolutionary sickness of nations" because of "the strength of her ancient customs." Even anti-British, ottantottist conservatives were often forced to admit that conservatism is, first of all, British. Thus Maistre in 1810 called the ancient, unwritten British constitution "the most complex unity and happy equilibrium of political powers that the world has ever seen."

Nonpolitical, Temperamental Conservatism. The conservative temperament may be, but need not be, identical with conservative politics or with right-wing economics; it may sometimes accompany so-called left-wing politics or economics. Regardless of his politics or economics, here are the two earmarks of the temperamental conservative: (1) a distrust of human nature, rootlessness, and untested innovations; (2) a trust in unbroken historical continuity and in some traditional framework to tame human nature. That framework may be inarticulate, religious, or cultural. Let us consider these three non-political aspects in turn.

Inarticulate Aspect. Some authorities on conservatism, a minority in France and a majority in England, consider conservatism an inarticulate state of mind, *not* at all an ideology. Liberalism argues, conservatism simply *is*. When conservatism becomes ideologized, logical, and self-conscious, then it resembles the liberal rationalists whom it opposes; it becomes paradoxically a mere liberalism of conservatism—that is, a mere doctrinaire theorizing of conservatism. According to this British approach, the logical deductive reasoning of Latin conservatives like Maistre is too doctrinaire, too eighteenth-century. It may even be generalized that the conservative mind does not like to generalize. Conservative theory is anti-theoretical. The liberal and rationalist mind consciously articulates abstract blueprints; the conservative mind unconsciously incarnates concrete traditions. Hence Newman defined Toryism as "loyalty to persons," and liberalism as loyalty to abstract slogans. Because conservatism embodies rather than argues, its best insights are not sustained theoretical works, as in the case of liberalism, but the quick thrust of epigrams; note those of Metternich, Disraeli, Tocqueville, Nietzsche, and Churchill in Part II (the document section).

Religious Aspect. Conservatism is usually associated with some traditional and established form of religion, whether as a credo to believe literally or as a framework historically valuable. After 1789, its appeal redoubled for those craving security in an age of chaos. The Catholic Church, because of its old roots in the monarchic middle ages, has appealed to more conservatives than any other religion. Himself a Church of England Protestant, Burke praised Catholicism as "the most effectual barrier" against radicalism. Such praise sounds as if motivated by secular expediency, not spiritual fervor. But a more spiritual Catholicism characterized the conservatism we shall examine in Newman and Cortés. Meanwhile conservatism has had no dearth of Protestant and strongly anti-clerical adherents also, notably John Adams. British conservatives, making a cult of their Church of England, combine Protestant and Catholic aspects of that complex institution.

Cultural Aspect. What in politics is the self-destructive vice of the extreme reactionary—his remoteness from the present—sometimes becomes his virtue in art. The remoteness may give him the perspective, the detachment that facilitates imaginative flights. Therefore, the most objectionable and bigoted reactionary may become in his art the most profound psychologist, the most sensitive moralist. Examples are Nietzsche, Balzac, Melville, Dostoyevsky, all discussed later. What counts most is not their sometimes embarrassing politics but their insights into the soul and into the wounds it suffers from a too-shallow kind of liberal material progress. Visionaries beyond politics, the cultural conservatives are forever weighing the moral debits against the material credits of a mechanical world. Cultural conservatism is a spiritual arithmetic: it calculates the price paid for progress.

Anti-Conservative Viewpoint. To assess a viewpoint so controversial as conservatism, the views of opponents must be balanced against those of proponents. Readers impressed by Burke's side of the debate ought also to read Paine's side, available in all libraries. Not as truths but merely in order to show what conservatives happen to believe, the present chapters state the main conservative arguments. These arguments may be regarded as mere hypotheses. They have been challenged by thoughtful liberals and radicals and, therefore, deserve to be questioned objectively by thoughtful readers. The student should ask himself at every step: to what extent is such and such a philosophy serious, and to what extent is it mere "fancy talk" concealing some selfish vested interest? By applying that question to each conservative argument and by also reading the books of the various anti-conservative rebels (Rousseau, Voltaire, Paine, Veblen, Marx), each student may assess the pros and cons of conservatism in his own free fashion. So doing, he may suddenly find himself working out his individual view not merely of politics but of the nature of man.

— 2 (General) —

"ARISTOCRAT" AND OTHER SPECIAL TERMS

Apriorism vs. Experience. This chapter attempts to clarify certain terms which conservative philosophers use with special emotion-charged, nondictionary meanings. They use the Latin term *"a priori"* for ideas deduced entirely from "prior" ideas, as opposed to ideas rooted in historical experience. The former are called "rootless," the latter "rooted"; the former "abstract," the latter "concrete." The chapter on Burke further develops these distinctions. Conservatives condemn, with the term "rationalist blueprints," the attempts of progressives to plan society in advance from pure reason instead of letting it grow "organically"—meaning: grow like a living plant, naturally and unconsciously, flowering up from the deep roots of tradition. Conservatives attribute the chaos and terror of the French Revolution to this *a priori* "eighteenth-century rationalism," an attribution rejected by many liberals.

Organic vs. Atomistic. Most European conservatives (see Coleridge, Chapter 5) view society as a single organism, having the special cohesiveness that comes only from being alive. They dismiss a liberal society as "atomistic," meaning disrupted dead atoms, held together merely mechanically. A society is allegedly made organic by religion, idealism, shared historical experiences like nationality, monarchy, or constitution, and the emotions of reverence, cooperation, loyalty. A society is allegedly made atomistic by materialism, class war, excessive *laisser-faire* economics, greedy profiteering, over analytical intellectuality, subversion of shared institutions, insistence on rights above duties, and the emotions of skepticism, cynicism, plebeian envy. Normally conservatives keep a sense of proportion about stressing organic unity. Except for the German romantic school (see Chapter 12) they do not carry it to the extreme where the individual becomes nothing, society everything. At that extreme we have no longer conservatism but totalitarian statism. If Germany's conservatives overstress organic unity, America's understress it. Furthermore, what popularly passes for "conservative" in America is often only a petrified right-wing of atomistic *laisser-faire* liberalism.

Liberty vs. Equality.   Do liberty and equality necessarily go together? Yes, proclaimed the French Revolution: *"liberté, égalité, fraternité!"* No, retorted conservatives; since people are unequally endowed, you can prevent inequality only by despotism—that is, by a Jacobin reign of terror to keep down those who are superior and to prevent them from using their liberty. In concrete instances, when conditions were morally and historically ripe, conservatives have sincerely supported equality also (see Chapter 6 on "Tory Democracy"). But they have never supported it as an abstraction, a cult, a fanatic and doctrinaire ism: "egalitarianism." The documents in Part II from John Adams, Burckhardt, Nietzsche, Tocqueville explore the menace of egalitarianism to liberty.

Aristocracy, Plutocracy, Democracy.   "Aristocracy" means rule by the best; definitions by Burke and Adams follow. "Plutocracy" means rule by the rich, often the newly rich, alleged by conservatives to be rootlessly commercial, without tradition and sense of honor. "Democracy," meaning rule by the people, is often despised by conservatives as a passionate mob agitated by revolutionists. But sometimes democracy is lauded by conservatives as a repository of folk traditions, whose simple wisdom is preferred to the sophistication of middle-class intellectuals.

Early conservatives, including both Burke and Maistre, did not believe democracy would work. A more favorable attitude toward democracy, provided it became rooted in some ancient traditional framework, characterized later conservatives like Tocqueville, Disraeli, Churchill. This eventual conservative acceptance of democracy led to a further distinction: direct vs. indirect democracy. In the former the people rule directly by referendum, plebiscite, petition, mob-pressure. In the latter they rule only indirectly via representatives, through whom the popular will gets safely filtered. This distinction divided liberals from conservatives when drawing up the American Constitution (see Chapter 14). For the conservative case against the tyranny of direct majorities, see the documents in Part II from Madison, Calhoun, Maine, Babbitt.

"Aristocracy" Defined by Burke and Adams. Let us hear from their own mouths what Burke and John Adams (President, 1797-1800) meant by "aristocrat," a word distrusted in modern democracies but used favorably by America's Federalist founders. In his *Appeal from the New Whigs to the Old,* 1791, Burke defined the word in terms of ancestral education and "unbought grace":

> To be bred in a place of estimation; to see nothing low and sordid from one's infancy; to be taught to respect one's self; to be habituated to the censorial inspection of the public eye; to look early to public opinion; to stand upon such elevated ground as to be enabled to take a large view of the widespread and infinitely diversified combinations of men and affairs in a large society; to have leisure to read, to reflect, to converse; to be enabled to draw the court and attention of the wise and learned wherever they are to be found; to be habituated in the pursuit of honor and duty . . . such are the elements that compose this unbought grace. . . .

In his *Defense of the Constitutions,* 1787-1788, Adams argued for inequality against the Jeffersonians: ". . . There are inequalities . . . which no human legislator ever can eradicate . . . because they have a natural and inevitable influence in society. . . . Children of illustrious families have generally greater advantages of education. . . . The characters of their ancestors described in history, or coming down by tradition, removes them farther from vulgar jealousy." In 1790 Adams added: "The nobles have been essential parties in the preservation of liberty . . . against kings and people. . . . By nobles, I mean not peculiarly an hereditary nobility, or any particular modification, but the natural and actual aristocracy among mankind . . . a division which nature has made and we cannot abolish. . . . It would not be true, but it would not be more egregiously false [*than attacking aristocracy*], to say that the people have waged everlasting war against the rights of men."

Historical Change in "Aristocrat." Whereas Burke was referring mainly to hereditary titled aristocracy, note that the Adams quotation also praised "natural" or untitled aristocracy. That distinction reflects a key difference between European and American conservatism. After middle-class merchants replaced aristocratic landowners in power, the conservative impulse to defend landed aristocracy often became sublimated into defending not the class itself but its ideals (honor, tradition, self-discipline). Thereupon the aristocratic ideals either were diffused among all classes or else were transferred to the new industrialist rulers. That transfer has been more characteristic of America's conservatism than Europe's, owing to our lack of stubborn feudal remnants.

Privilege Justified. The conservative apologist cannot deny that his élite has more privileges than the rest of the population. These privileges did not require any long philosophical justification in the days when aristocracy still felt relatively unthreatened. Hence the major philosophies of conservatism were devised only *after* the French Revolution and its egalitarian rationalism threatened aristocratic traditionalism all over the globe. Thereafter, conservatives justified aristocratic privileges by elaborating the old concept of *noblesse oblige*. That concept means: a noble class, by having more privileges than others, feels ethically "obliged" to perform more duties also. These added duties have included: public services, public leadership, moral example, the valuable hereditary civil service of British nobles, the intellectual and artistic patronage of the royal French court, the ceremonious symbolizing by noblemen of the historic, political, and religious heritages of their countries.

"Let governments govern," argued the Austrian Prince Metternich. Restore "throne and altar," argued the French-Italian Count de Maistre. Bask reverently in the shade of the "great oaks" of aristocracy, exhorted Burke, echoed by Disraeli. But what when one of its great oaks behaves, instead, like a crass weed? At that point conservatism becomes vulnerable to liberal and egalitarian attacks on privilege; in such cases *noblesse* does not *oblige*. Consequently, in our modern democracies, conservatives no longer state explicitly that defense of aristocratic privilege which was their historical origin. That defense is vulnerable; it would "lose votes." Yet it is still there implicitly. It still serves to differentiate conservatives from liberals on the unconscious or unwritten level even when, as so often today, their programs agree on the conscious or written level.

— 3 (General) —

THE GREAT REVERSAL: FROM INTERNATIONALISM TO NATIONALISM

Nationalism Becomes Conservative Weapon. The impact of historical evolution upon conservative ideas has already been observed in the changing content of "aristo-crat." A second change, equally important for understanding why conservatives disagree with one another, was from aristocratic internationalism to middle-class nationalism. Let us refer to it hereafter as the Great Reversal. Most (not all) conservatives were international-ists during 1789-1848, nationalists after 1870. For con-crete examples of internationalist conservatism, note the chapters on Maistre, Cortés, Metternich; for nationalist conservatism, those on Barrès and on Germany (Trei-tschke). During 1815-1848, the sentiment of nationalism was used by rebels out of power. They used it to disrupt the domestic *status quo* (especially in ethnically mixed Austria) and to promote democratic change. During 1870-1914, nationalism was used by governments in power. They used it to stabilize the domestic *status quo* and to prevent democratic social change.

Pride in nationality was essential from the start to many conservative philosophers, notably Burke. But it was essential among other ancestral traditions, not as the only one. Nationalism differed from conservatism in that it conserved only one of man's several historical roots. When all other roots and loyalties, including religion, ethics, and humanity, were sacrificed to the nationalist root, then a narrow fanaticism resulted. Examples were Treitschke in Germany, Barrès in France, Rudyard Kipling (1865-1936) partly, in England. The post-1945 trend among philosophical conservatives regards the Prussian militarism of Bismarck and the racial self-worship of nationalist conservatives like Barrès as an anti-Christian, pagan idolatry. The Christian religion itself, so basic to conservatives, is by definition internationalist.

Middle-class Origins. Originally nationalism, as expressed in the revolutions of the 1820's and 1848, was not a mass movement at all. It was a movement of middle-class intellectuals (for example, the German romantic school of the early 1800's). They were using nationalism as a reaction against the radical internationalism of the French invader and also against conservative aristocratic cosmopolitanism, from which the middle class felt excluded. Through education and the press, nationalism thereafter spread from its educated middle-class founders to the masses, above all to the lower middle classes in whom nationalism found its staunchest adherents. These generalizations are based on such current authorities on nationalism as Carlton J. H. Hayes, Hans Kohn, Boyd Shafer, Louis L. Snyder.

Radicals Adopt Internationalism. The Great Reversal of conservatism was accompanied by a Great Reversal in the opposite direction among revolutionists. During 1815-1848, the line-up seemed clear enough: international aristocratic conservatism versus nationalist middle-class liberalism. The line-up was disrupted when Italy and Germany achieved a nationalistic unity not from below but from above and with conservative monarchies. As conservatives became nationalists and became allied with the middle class, revolutionists became internationalists. Back in 1848, the internationalist *Communist Manifesto* of Marx and Engels had evoked scant response. By the 1870's, as conservatives became identified with nationalism, the international radicalism of Marxism was found to command a huge internationalist movement of workers and intellectuals all over Europe.

Nationalism Out of Control. Though unleashed by the middle classes, mass nationalism could no longer be controlled by them once it exploded into the fever heat of twentieth-century fascism and nazism, whose ruling class was a new type of totalitarian demagogue. The

Italian Prime Minister of Piedmont-Sardinia, Camillo di Cavour (1810-1861), and the Prussian Prime Minister Otto von Bismarck (1815-1898), by retaining the traditional framework of monarchy and aristocracy, were still able to control mass nationalism. It was their tool for disrupting the Austrian empire and founding the nationalist monarchies of Italy and Germany, 1861 and 1871. Cavour and Bismarck could still use nationalism rather than be used by it. They were the last great statesmen to be able to do so. A king of Italy in 1922, a president of Germany in 1933 could do so no longer. Instead, the new totalitarian demagogue moved to the center of the stage. Conservative hopes that nationalism would stabilize the *status quo* against revolutions were dashed when, instead, it brought two world wars, causing revolutions, social chaos, and the moral chaos of racist atrocities.

Back to Internationalism. After World War II, the three leading conservative statesmen—the German Chancellor Konrad Adenauer (1876-   ), the British Prime Minister Winston Churchill (1874-   ), the Italian Premier Alcide De Gasperi (1881-1954)—turned back to internationalism and to Western union and away from isolationism. Today many conservatives are reversing the Great Reversal, partly because they need an international barrier against Soviet aggression. The anti-communist conservative internationalism of Churchill, Adenauer, and De Gasperi after World War II paralleled, though on a more democratic basis, the anti-Jacobin conservative internationalism of Metternich, Castlereagh, and Talleyrand after 1815. But such short-run material expediency may not entirely explain the return of conservatives in the 1950's to their original internationalist roots. There may also be a long-run ethical explanation: Christianity.

II BRITISH

— 4 —

BURKE

Personal Background. Edmund Burke (1729-1797) founded modern conservatism. Almost singlehanded, he turned the intellectual tide from a rationalist contempt for the past to a traditionalist reverence for it. He was born in Dublin, a middle-class Irishman, his father Protestant, his mother Catholic, the boy Protestant. He loved old England, its established Anglican Church and its nobility, with a plebeian outsider's passion, unmatched by anyone born in England itself. Eighteenth-century London drew bright and poor young Irishmen and Scotsmen hoping for a noble patron; it drew Burke in 1750. In 1765 he became private secretary to the Marquis of Rockingham, the nobleman who then headed the Whig party, and entered parliament the same year. Burke rapidly became the most persuasive orator, the most influential philosophical defender of the aristocratic and liberty-loving ideals of the Whig landowners.

Eighteenth-century Parliament. In those days the two rival parties, Whigs and Tories, did not really differ ideologically. Both were controlled by the same landed gentry. They did, however, partly differ about parliament; the Whigs and Burke defended its rights (as established in 1688) against the innovating encroachments of their semi-alien Teutonic King, George III (House of Hanover). Not that the parliament of Burke's day was democratic or responsible to the people. Parliament was an exclusive gentlemen's club for Whig and Tory landed noblemen and their protégés. They were elected by a limited suffrage excluding the masses and even most of the middle classes. Yet modern democracies may well envy the vigorous free speech and unlimited free debate of Burke's aristocratic parliament, a freedom unequalled by modern mass parliaments, dependent on mass elections and mass demagogy.

Feudal Origins of Liberty. According to conservative historians, parliamentary and civil liberties were created not by modern liberal democracy but by medieval feudalism, not by equality but by privilege. These free institutions—Magna Cartas, constitutions, Witens, Dumas, and parliaments—were originally founded and bled for by medieval noblemen, fighting selfishly and magnificently for their historic rights against both kinds of tyranny, the tyranny of kings and the tyranny of the conformist masses. Modern democracy merely inherited from feudalism that sacredness of individual liberty and then, so to speak, mass-produced it. Democracy changed liberty from an individual privilege to a general right, thereby gaining in quantity of freedom but losing in quality of freedom—that is, losing in the creative intensity of earlier aristocracies, such as Elizabethan England, the British Parliament before 1832, Renaissance Italy, or the brilliant French court that fostered Racine, Corneille, Molière. The eighteenth-century "rotten boroughs," those much-denounced electoral seats controlled by a single noble family, sent into parliament great, freedom-defending statesmen like Pitt, Burke, Sheridan. Such men had intellectual standards allegedly too high to be elected with equal frequency to any democratic parliament, based on mass appeals. Thus considered, feudal privilege and aristocratic non-conformist individualism may be the true root of liberty; a leveling, democratic egalitarianism would then be the true foe of liberty. Many leading authorities reject this undemocratic hypothesis; wrong or right, it is essential to the conservative temperament.

1776 vs. 1789. In the light of that hypothesis, it was not inconsistent, as Paine charged, but consistent for Burke to defend the moderate American Revolution of 1776 and to attack the radical French Revolution of 1789. Burke interpreted the former as led by aristocratic Whig gentlemen like Washington, fighting not for newfangled innovations but for traditional rights against royal usurpation. The French Revolution he saw as a usurpation by mobs and unrooted intellectuals against "tradition" and hence (by his association of those two terms) against "liberty"—liberty being contrasted by him with the French Revolution's stress on equality.

Burke's pro-American speeches included "On Concilia-
tion with the Colonies," 1775, and "On American Taxation," 1777. His *Reflections on the Revolution in France,*
1790, has been called "the most influential pamphlet ever
written." It is also the best single essay on conservatism,
the source of most conservative arguments ever after,
and an uncannily accurate prophecy. (*See Document
No. 1.*) Its early date of 1790, at a time when most
intellectuals still had faith in the new dawn in France,
is all the more remarkable when one considers that the
Revolution was then still a splendid success on the surface and had not yet entered its phase of terror and
dictatorship. Burke predicted that phase not by any lucky,
blind guess but by analyzing its lack of historical roots.

Contract with the Past. Burke distinguished between the two Revolutions by the criterion of fidelity
to the past. That criterion leads to the question: what
relationship should the present have with the past? Here
we come to the core of Burke and conservatism: fear of
rootlessness. Rousseau's *Social Contract* of 1762 had
favored a contract merely among the living, arranging
government for their mutual benefit. Burke, instead,
argued: "Society is indeed a contract. . . . [*But*] as the
ends of such a partnership cannot be obtained in many
generations, it becomes a partnership not only between
those who are living but between those who are living,
those who are dead, and those who are to be born. . . .
Changing the state as often as there are floating fancies,
. . . no one generation could link with the other. Men
would be little better than the flies of a summer." The
comparison with summer-flies illustrates Burke's characteristic talent (reflecting his youthful praise of "sublime
poetry") for political use of striking literary metaphors.
Contrast this poetic love for past generations with the
rationalist hostility of the most influential anti-conservative
of modern times, Karl Marx: "The legacy of the dead
generations weighs like a nightmare upon the brains of
the living."

But for Burke the contract is with "the future" as
well as with the past. Unlike Maistre, Burke urges evolutionary improvements: "A disposition to preserve and
an ability to improve, taken together, would be my
standard of a statesman." That sentence remains the
perfect definition of the evolutionary kind of conservative.

The statesman's double function is, he adds, "at once to preserve and to reform." In contrast, the liberal one-sidedly overemphasizes the reforming half of that double function, while the Maistre-style conservative over-emphasizes the preserving half.

Natural vs. Prescriptive Rights. Burke was defending not conservatism in the abstract but one concrete instance of it, the unwritten British Constitution. He seemed more concerned with winning the defense than with winning it consistently. Sometimes he justified that Constitution by "natural rights"; more often by "prescriptive right." "Natural rights" meant: a universal code external to any given constitution. "Prescriptive right" meant: a local code inherent in it and "prescribed" by its sheer age, its sheer act of being there. Sometimes he said natural rights preceded the Constitution and gave it "latent wisdom." But when arguing against French rationalists, who would justify their own revolutionary constitution by natural rights, he said instead and more typically: "Our Constitution is a prescriptive constitution [*whose*] . . . sole authority is that it has existed time out of mind . . . without any reference whatever to any other more general or prior right." The latest research of the philosopher Leo Strauss confirms that Burke never resolved that contradiction. (Burke, *Works,* London, 1854-1857; II, 306, 359, 443; III, 110, 112; VI, 146; vs. Strauss, *Natural Right and History,* Chicago, 1953, pp. 318-319.)

Since all traditions cannot be equally perfect and may contradict each other, what mechanism is to weed out the inferior ones? Sometimes he implied the universal natural rights of Christianity would do the weeding, as opposed to the universal natural rights of unreligious rationalists. More often he ignored both kinds of natural rights and left the weeding to the expediency of time: "The individual is foolish; the multitude for the moment is foolish, when they act without deliberation; but the species is wise; and when time is given to it, as a species it almost always acts right."

Champion of Free Mind. Here is a concrete chronology of Burke's defense of certain liberties. In 1771, he defended freedom of speech in debating the law of libel and defended ceding to the press the right of reporting parliamentary debates. In 1773, he supported relieving Protestant Dissenters from the Anglican Test Act on grounds of its limiting intellectual freedom. In 1775, he vainly urged conciliating the revolting American colonists. In 1776, he twice supported further motions for conciliating the colonists, though the war had already begun. In 1778, he attacked use of Indians against the colonists and supported measures to remove penalities on Catholics. In 1786, 1788, and again 1794, he made leading speeches to impeach Warren Hastings for violating the traditional rights of his colonial subjects in India.

The position of Burke in all the above instances would also be endorsed by modern liberal democrats. But at the same time, he was attacking the ability of the masses and the demand for giving them new liberties and for letting them vote. Was he being inconsistent, as charged? Yes, from the viewpoint of liberal democrats, the viewpoint of liberty *plus* democracy. No, from his own viewpoint of liberty *versus* democracy. With some exceptions, the following distinctions hold: he would rather defend intellectual liberties (free press, free religion) than mass liberties; he would rather defend habitual or constitutional liberties (including those of colonials) than new ones or *a priori* ones; he would rather defend the liberties of an élite intellectually capable of using them responsibly, namely, parliament, than the liberties of allegedly irresponsible masses. He defended the liberties *even* of the masses if they were time-tested rights. But the French Revolution confirmed his fear of untested new rights. That position locates his constitutionalist conservatism midway between liberal democrats (Jefferson) and authoritarian conservatives (Maistre). When embittered, Burke sometimes fluctuated to the far right (*Letters On A Regicide Peace,* 1796-1797). But normally, most authorities agree, he stuck to the middle road.

Middle Road: Experience, Not Theories. As the man of the middle road, Burke attacked not solely the democratic masses but likewise the usurpations of King George III. The same Burke who attacked the French Revolution in 1789, attacked the slave trade one year earlier. In May, 1788, he demanded the total abolition of slavery, hardly the demand of a foe of liberty and social change. "A state without the means of some change is without the means of its conservation"—that sentence of 1790 best expressed his most lasting achievement: the synthesis of conservatism with evolution. He exalted the allegedly "British" middle road of compromise over the allegedly "French" propensity for extreme doctrinaire theories. So doing, he helped overthrow eighteenth-century rationalism, whose trend was toward theorizing. Yet he cannot be dismissed as simply an anti-rational romantic (except for some early writings of 1756). He had his own kind of reasonableness; its base was neither deductive rationalism nor an instinct-exalting romanticism but a playing by ear, based on experience.

"Prudence" and "Prejudice." Though he is sometimes called "romantic" and sometimes was, yet one cannot imagine any romanticist praising sober common sense and prudence as Burke did in *An Appeal from the New to the Old Whigs,* August, 1791: "One sure symptom of an ill-conducted state is the propensity of the people to theories. The lines of morality are not like ideal lines of mathematics. They admit of exceptions; they demand modifications . . . not made by the process of logic, but by the rule of prudence. Prudence is not only first in rank of the virtues political and moral, but she is the director. . . ." Thus his "prudence" differed equally from French rationalism and from the anti-rational intuitions of German romanticism.

British prudence, he believed, does carry reason far enough to let an élite introduce moderate liberal reforms from above—but not far enough to unleash from below the chaotic masses of the population or to disrobe society: "All the pleasing illusions, which made power gentle and obedience liberal, which harmonized the different shades of life . . . are to be dissolved by this new conquering empire of light and reason." Burke shocked his century by his brutal frankness in defending "illusions" and "prejudices" as socially necessary. Thereby he was being not so much a cynic as one of the only old-fashioned Christians among eighteenth-century intellectuals. He was an old-fashioned Christian in the sense of believing man innately depraved, innately steeped in Original Sin, incapable of bettering himself by his feeble reason. So defined, man could only be tamed by following an ethically trained élite and by education in "prejudices," such as family, religion, aristocracy. He called landed aristocrats "the great oaks" and "proper chieftains," provided they tempered their rule by a spirit of timely reform from above and remained within the constitutional framework. In contrast with what he deemed the rootless skepticism of a Voltaire and the social chaos of a Rousseau, Burke defended the Church of England for its political as well as religious function: "To keep moral, civil, and political bonds together binding human understanding."

A Temperament, Not a Philosophy. Burke was too much the practical man of action, expediently winning immediate battles, to leave his heirs any universal philosophy: "No rational man ever did govern himself by abstractions or universals." His rival intellectual heirs are still arguing about what he meant. Not only conservatives but liberals, socialists (Harold Laski), and neo-Thomist Catholics have sometimes also claimed him. All can cite his inconsistent scripture to support their rival claims. Yet even if men disagree about what the Burkean philosophy means, they can agree about what the Burkean temperament means: "Rage and frenzy will pull down more in half an hour than prudence, deliberation, and foresight can build up in one hundred years. A spirit of innovation is generally the result of a selfish temper." The logic of formulas can predict how dead chemicals will act but not how living humans will act. Therefore, the Burkean temperament tests institutions by experience, not by prior formulas. That temperament is more important for conservatism than his or any other philosophy. British conservatives never tire of stressing that theirs is a nonpolitical and nonphilosophical way of life, not a definable political philosophy like Marxism, fascism, or eighteenth-century French liberalism.

Despite Burke's philosophical contradiction between inner and outer kinds of justification, the Burkean temperament assumes a simultaneous combination of both: values are external in origin, namely in the universal religion of Christianity, but are ineffective abstractions unless meanwhile rooted internally in some concrete historic past. That same combination—a particularized universality—has also increasingly become the aim of the best current liberal thought, in contrast with the unchastened, more abstract liberals who once were duped by the false dawns of 1789 or 1917. Today the more chastened liberals and the more moderate conservatives have become parallel lines meeting not in infinity but in

Burke. They share a common resistance to the abstract doctrinaires and unethical despots of left or right extremes.

Liberal Case Against Burke. Not only have conservatives idolized Burke; even a leading liberal historian, Thomas Babington Macaulay (1800-1859), called him the greatest man since Milton. What did his opponents reply to all this? Paine's rebuttal of 1791 accused him of excessive pessimism about democracy and the common man. Supposedly that pessimism made Burke slander the French Revolution, which was nobly spreading liberty and equality by the enlightened use of pure reason, backed by a little wholesome prodding from the bayonet and the guillotine. Less naive anti-Burkeans charge him with immoral expediency, kowtowing to nobles, and a pathological fear of disorder. All three charges are found in the ablest modern case against Burke (Dr. Gertrude Himmelfarb in *The Twentieth Century,* London, May 1953):

> Where Rousseau was solicitous of a future democratic state, Burke was interested only in making impregnable the existing aristocratic one. . . . Prescription and presumption were, of course, admirably suited to the interests of the aristocracy, and it is strange to find so many commentators soberly defending the thesis that Burke, the employee of the most aristocratic faction of the Whig party, stood for some sort of popular government. . . . Only this extraordinary facility for disguise . . . can account for the high esteem Edmund Burke has enjoyed. . . . He cared as little as the serpent where he attacked or how; the important thing was that the attack succeeded. . . . He and fear were born, as twins, together. . . . Fear of disorder pursued Burke so far as to convince him that liberty could be acceptable [*only*] as long as it was "liberty with order."

Maine (1822-1888). No consistent philosopher, Burke left the systematizing of his ideas to disciples of more talent, less genius, notably Sir Henry Maine. Maine's *Popular Government,* 1885, systematized the Burkean approach into a consistent philosophy, gave it a scholarly basis, and applied it to the post-Burkean problems of modern industrialism. Distrusting universal suffrage and the tyranny of the majority, Maine argued that you cannot have liberty and equality simultaneously and preferred the former. Liberty and civilization "cannot be disentangled" from private property, the source of individual rights; collective property or socialism means "the tyranny of the majority." Opponents countered: did he not admit that America and England had liberty despite having democracy? Maine's reply: true enough, but only because of unique historical conditions and because they were indirect democracies. Their constitutional checks prevented majority tyranny: "By a wise constitution, democracy may be made nearly as calm as water in a great artificial reservoir; but if there is a weak point anywhere in the structure, the mighty forces which it controls will burst through and spread destruction." (*See Document No. 21.*)

— 5 (British) —

COLERIDGE, CARLYLE, NEWMAN

Where Culture and Politics Overlap. The present chapter deals with those critics of material progress—Coleridge the most important one—who were defined on pages 16-17 as "cultural conservatives." Coleridge and Carlyle were also active politically, influencing the Conservative party. Therefore, they may almost as well be classified as political conservatives. What they really represent is the area where both categories overlap. Because conservatism stresses concrete emotional loyalties more than abstract theories, it overlaps more frequently with poetry (that crystallization of the emotional and the concrete) than do any other political isms. Four leading conservatives of nineteenth-century England were also leading poets: Samuel Coleridge (1772-1834), William Wordsworth (1770-1850), John Newman (1801-1890), Matthew Arnold (1822-1888). Newman's poem of 1833, "Lead, Kindly Light," is still a favorite hymn; the verse of the three others is even more familiar than their prose.

Disillusioned with Revolution. Coleridge and

Wordsworth ended as "mixed" conservatives: sometimes ottantottist, sometimes Burkean. But they began as utopian liberals supporting the French Revolution. Wordsworth spoke for a whole generation of European intellectuals with his famous salute to the new dawn in France: "Bliss was it in that dawn to be alive, but to be young was very heaven." Disillusionment followed. Coleridge and Wordsworth reacted from liberalism and rationalism to traditional monarchy and church of England. The same pattern in the twentieth century has created the standard figure of the disillusioned ex-communist intellectual, reacting violently against that Russian pseudo-dawn when "to be young was very heaven."

Coleridge's Writings. In 1798 Wordsworth and Coleridge published their joint book of poems, *Lyrical Ballads.* It marked the revolt of the human heart against abstract eighteenth-century rationalists; thereby it helped set a new philosophical climate. Conservatism was permanently influenced towards greater depth and imagination by Coleridge's prose works: *Lay Sermons,* 1816; *Biographia Literaria,* 1817; *Philosophical Lectures,* 1818-1819; *Aids to Reflection,* 1825; and his various *Letters* and *Table Talk.* Sixty notebooks of his chaotic but fascinating jottings, covering 1794-1834, are still to be published in eight volumes in the 1950's. Influential indirectly, by molding the minds of university students who later became national leaders, were his public lectures. He fulfilled his genius only in his magnetic conversations; his writings remained incomplete, fragmentary. His insights were not worked out in sustained volumes but came in short, epigrammatic flashes. (*See Document 6.*)

Class Lines Justified. According to Coleridge, society divided its functions among different "class orders." Each class had its valuable function, but this did not necessarily include the right to vote and rule. That right was best left to an ethically trained aristocracy, functioning within the strict lawful limits of parliament. No class war; all classes must coöperate harmoniously within the "organic" unity of that revered British constitution. His greatest influence on practical politics was via Disraeli and other Tory leaders. They learned from Coleridge to justify class differences philosophically, to find spiritual values in the once-despised Middle Ages, and to despise instead the utilitarian values of the rising capitalist class, which took over the Whig party from its earlier Burkean noblemen.

No Vote for "Shopkeepers." According to the one-sided allegations of Coleridgeans, the businessman was inherently subversive: a wild-eyed radical at best, he gnawed at the foundations of Christian monarchy by substituting a new-fangled, un-Christian religion known as economic profit. ("Economics is the gospel of Mammon" was John Ruskin's very Coleridgean definition.) Such un-British activities must be put down by denying this strange new commercial class enough votes to control Parliament. Thus Coleridge, defining "shopkeepers" as "the least patriotic and the least conservative" class, fought against the Whig Reform Bill of 1832, which gave so many of them the right to vote.

Coleridge vs. Burke. Coleridge is considered the "purest" of all conservatives, never compromising with material self-interest. Burke's philosophy was morally compromised by opportunistic party politics. In an otherwise admiring essay of 1809, Coleridge objected to Burke's unnecessary "compromise of greatness with meanness" and quoted Oliver Goldsmith's verdict on Burke: "Who, born for the universe, narrowed his mind/ And to party gave up what was meant for mankind." Never having been so radical when young, Burke was never so reactionary when old as Coleridge and Wordsworth; Burke was also more practical, less vapidly obscure than Coleridge at his worst. But Burke never approached the penetrating poetic intuitions of Coleridge at his best. For example, Coleridge, in his *France: An Ode* of 1798, condensed into just a few lines of poetry what Burke had taken so much longer to say about the same Revolution:

> When France in wrath her giant-limbs upreared, . . .
> Stamped her strong foot and said she would be free,
> Bear witness for me, how I hoped and feared! . . .
> The Sensual and the Dark rebel in vain,
> Slaves by their own compulsion! In mad game
> They burst their manacles and wear the name
> Of freedom, graven on a heavier chain!

Society Organic. Coleridge deemed society organic, not atomistic; *laisser-faire* liberals fatally dissected its living whole by overstressing its separate parts. An encounter between Coleridge and a certain liberal Miss Martineau epitomized that debate. "You seem," said Coleridge, "to regard society as an aggregate of individuals." She answered, "Of course, I do." *In Victorian England,* G. M. Young commented: "There is much history implicit in that encounter, and by 1850 Coleridge had won. . . . It was inevitable that, in a generation . . . bemused by Coleridge, the corporate and sacramental aspect of the Church should re-emerge and . . . feelings of beauty, antiquity, and mystery." With a seemingly simple aphorism—"Persons are not things"—Coleridge refuted a century of rationalist planners, who had tried to rearrange "persons" into the neat, mathematical patterns of "things." Not being "things," the "persons" either broke or hit back; hence the agony of Europe since the rationalist French Revolution.

Bentham vs. Coleridge. Nineteenth-century intellectuals felt they had to choose between Jeremy Bentham (1748-1832), founder of "utilitarianism," and Coleridge. The British scholar, R. J. White, defined their "essential difference" as "the difference between the man [*Bentham*] who takes social institutions as so many pieces of furniture that can be moved around, rearranged, refashioned, or even chopped up for firewood, and the man [*Coleridge*] who sees them as elements in the total concrete experience of a people—not as the furniture of life, but as life itself." Coleridge had the deeper psychological appeal; thus the liberal rationalist, John Stuart Mill, partly moved from Bentham to Coleridge in order to find emotional relief for a nervous breakdown caused by a childhood of dry, unemotional Benthamism. The Benthamites, then called "philosophical radicals," also differed from Coleridge on history and religion. "History, to the Benthamites a dusty record of the crimes and follies of mankind, was to Coleridge an inspiring chronicle of the gradual unfolding of society" (Michael Packe, *Life of John Stuart Mill*). "Religion," said Coleridge, and not Benthamite utility, "is and ever has been the center of gravity."

The Case for Coleridge: Inner Growth. Coleridge defined the eternal Jacobin temperament as the illusion that "happiness depends on forms of government" and on programs of mere politics. That definition implied an exciting new theory of psychology. It contrasted inner and outer change. Outer change was conscious, material, purposeful. Inner change was unconscious, spiritual, quietly growing. Man's outer life was rootless and secular; it craved democracy and a written constitution. Man's inner life was traditional and religious; it craved a landed aristocracy, an established church, and an unwritten constitution. Outer progressive reforms, such as written constitutions and articulate party programs, were mere froth compared to the inarticulate inner growth. Inner growth was slow but organic; Coleridge deemed it deep and lasting. The outer growth of politics and of consciously contrived efforts was quicker and noisier but dead and mechanical; he deemed it shallow and temporary. Coleridgean conservatism seems exceeded only by Nietzsche in its understanding, a century before Sigmund Freud, of the unconscious mind.

Case Against Coleridge.   The utilitarian case against Coleridge made the following points. The conservative preference of country to city and of aristocrat to plutocrat is irrational prejudice. The original aristocrats were robber barons as upstart as any *nouveau riche*. The latter, given time enough, can become just as civilized as any aristocrat and more productive. No rural aristocrat has done so much for economic living standards and also for cultural projects as the benevolent industrialist and emancipated workingman of the big city.

More bitter opponents of Coleridge added a more personal attack, somewhat as follows. The incomprehensible opium-dreams of a senile mystic were being exploited by titled parasites, bigoted clergymen, and outdated Tories. The purpose was to cheat the sane and sturdy British shopkeeper of his leading role by slandering him and by restricting his right to vote. Yet a leading role, replacing the older order, was the logical right of that solid burgher in a liberated society, a society based not on religion nor beauty nor old custom but on efficiency, usefulness, and economics.

Carlyle: Part Proto-Fascist, Part Humanitarian. Thomas Carlyle (1795-1881) was the most vigorous and influential polemicist of the Victorian age. Certain of his teachings anticipated fascism: his anti-Semitic racism, his cult of power and of dictatorial military heroes. These nonconservative elements he partly derived from his admiration of two different aspects of Germany: its Prussianism, its romanticism. Sometimes he reads less like a British conservative than a translation from the German. Later he became a favorite of the Nazis; the last book Hitler read before his death in the bunker in Berlin was Carlyle's admiring biography of Prussia's Frederick the Great. But Carlyle's social conscience to aid the poor was just as basic as his brutal fascist-style outbursts. He gave British conservatism a humanitarianism that *laisserfaire* liberals in those days lacked. His "hero" in the Tory party was the humane Robert Peel (1788-1850).

Medievalism vs. Cash Nexus. Carlyle advocated class unity, not class war; traditional roots; an aristocracy not of economic greed but of public service; a society not atomistic but organic; spiritual medievalism as against materialistic "cash-nexus." By "cash-nexus" he meant a relationship based merely on economic gain. He preferred a relationship based on honor, loyalty, personal affection, all those more human qualities which conservatives cherish (against both capitalist and socialist materialists) as Burke's "unbought grace of life." These conservative ideals were elaborated in Carlyle's books, *Sartor Resartus,* 1833-1834; *On Heroes,* 1841; *Past and Present,* 1843. Like so many conservatives (Burke, Maistre, Tocqueville, Taine), Carlyle published his own particular *History of the French Revolution,* 1837; a malicious wit labelled it "a historical novel." The two parts of *Past and Present* (*see Document 14*) contrasted a present of starvation and agitation, known as "the hungry '40's," with an idealized past. In *Past,* he lauded a medieval monastery as organic, disciplined, just. In *Present,* he indicted democratic mobs and plutocratic profiteers for their cashnexus selfishness. He urged both to ennoble their natures by becoming respectively "captains of industry" and "a workingman aristocracy"; these two coined phrases typified his heroic, sometimes mock-heroic outlook and style.

Other phrases coined first in his books were "redtape"; "an honest day's work for an honest day's wage"; "democracy is the absence of a hero to worship"; democratic voters are "full of beer and balderadash." Showing his American friend, the philosopher Ralph Waldo Emerson, a session of Parliament, Carlyle exclaimed scornfully: "Do you believe in the devil now?" One cannot imagine such scorn from more traditional British conservatives like Burke and Churchill; such men loved Parliament and preferred its constitutional rule to Carlyle's imported Germanic "*Fuehrers.*" Carlyle trod more traditional Tory ground when he expounded the conservative thesis that inarticulate, inner spiritual laws are more decisive than articulate, outer written laws. He was at his ethical and literary best when urging his readers to "reform them- selves first if they want England reformed."

Today Carlyle's influence has dwindled. His bombastic, bullying style repels; not he but Coleridge in England, Tocqueville in France, Irving Babbitt in America are today deemed the most perceptive mentors of intellec- tual Toryism. But Carlyle's influence was once so en- ormous that one of America's ablest scholars, Emery Neff, in *Carlyle and Mill,* saw this pair as the main repre- sentatives of all British conservatism and liberalism re- spectively.

Oxford Movement. The Oxford Movement stood for religious conservatism within the Anglican Church, the church which since Henry VIII has been the estab- lished "Church of England." The movement began at Oxford, England in 1833 when John Keble (1792-1866) preached his "apostasy sermon." It ended, in its original unified form, in 1845 when John Newman quit its Angli- can ranks to join the Church of Rome. The movement was led by Keble, Newman, Edward Pusey, and others. During 1833-1841, they published their influential "Tracts for the Times," attacking "the advance of liberalism" in religion. They aimed to lead the Anglican Church—and society in general— back to dogma, medieval spirituality, and the poetic rituals lost during the Protestant Reforma- tion. Dogma, ritual, poetry, tradition, and Oxford were their common denominators. Keble and Newman both published verse; both taught at tradition-loving Oxford University, where Keble was professor of poetry. Both loathed liberalism and social change. Thereby they gave this primarily religious movement a traditionalist Tory bias in the secondary field of politics also.

Newman on Original Sin. In contrast with Keble, some leaders of the Oxford Movement, a minority, be- came Roman Catholic. Newman (*see Document 18*) was their spokesman. His conversion was much denounced, much praised; it began in 1841, was officially consum- mated in 1845. In 1879 Pope Leo XIII appointed him

Cardinal. He took that occasion to reaffirm publicly his lifelong battle against what he called "liberalism in religion."

Historically considered, Newman belongs to the line of great Christian pessimists. That line goes back to Saint Augustine. It goes forward not only to Catholics like Cortés but to such great Protestant religious philosophers as the Danish Søren Kierkegaard (1819-1855), the Swiss Karl Barth (1886-   ), the American Reinhold Niebuhr (1892-   ). Their common denominator is a stress on human depravity, on the difficulty of human nature blue-printing progress for itself. Distrusting human nature, most conservatives believe in Original Sin at least meta-phorically. Newman believed not metaphorically but liter-ally. In his autobiography he argued that the sinfulness of "fierce wilful human nature" required a "breakwater against the deluge." For him, the "breakwater" was the Church of Rome. For others, it may be a different insti-tution. But all conservatives agree that some breakwater is needed against the mob chaos outside us and inside us. The influence of his autobiography, *Apologia Pro Vita Sua*, 1864, has not been restricted to Catholics. Other readers, too, owe to that beautifully written book a new fascination with traditional dogma of whatever creed.

Matthew Arnold. A stress on historical continuity also marked Matthew Arnold. His most influential book was *Culture and Anarchy*, 1869. It performed in educa-tion and culture the same conservative protest against the new rootless plutocracy that Newman performed in religion, Coleridge in philosophy, Disraeli in politics. Long before Sinclair Lewis was born, Arnold's book satirized as "the philistine" the same uncultured plutocratic type known in America as "Babbitt." Arnold urged a return to the value-transmitting literary classics of the past.

The Anti-Industrial Theme. The conservatives of this chapter all have in common a sensitive temperament reacting, through culture or through religion, against the industrial revolution. Another example is the anti-pluto-cratic philosopher of art, John Ruskin (1819-1900), partly a conservative medievalist, partly a Christian social-ist. Some liberals picture conservatives as thick-skinned brutes, selfishly defending their own lucrative *status quo*. In contrast with this stereotype, genuine conservatives like Coleridge and Newman typify all the thin-skinned idealists, artists, and dreamers who conserve man's traditional religious and aesthetic magic against the disenchantment that follows industrialism. Thus argue cultural conservatives. Opponents argue: financed by those slandered but in reality public-spirited creatures known as plutocrats, modern industrialism need not be sordid; it can provide energies for welfare and beauty unequalled by any past age.

The diversity of conservative attitudes is shown by the fact that popular parlance in America calls two opposite groups "conservative": (1) the efficient modernism, cash-nexus selfishness, and atomistic society of the plutocrats; (2) the inefficient medievalism, anti-plutocratic idealism, and organic society of Coleridge, Carlyle, Newman, Ruskin. Yet both usages of "conservatism" have a partly unifying common denominator: both distrust the masses, prefer an established élitist authority, and distrust the abstract radical blueprints of utopians and of statists.

— 6 (British) —

TORY DEMOCRACY: DISRAELI AND CHURCHILL

Beyond Burke. Benjamin Disraeli (1804-1881) and Winston Churchill (1874-   ), the two most famous prime ministers produced by the British Conservative party, were both partly disciples of Burke. (Disraeli called Burke's writings "divine effusions.") But they moved two steps beyond Burke when they adopted greater imperialism and greater democracy. So doing, they became less and more democratic than he: less democratic in their treatment of colonial areas and more democratic at home. As imperialists, they would not have supported Burke's attacks on British high-handedness in India. As a believer in restricting the vote to a small élite at home, Burke would not have shared their "Tory democracy," namely, their wooing of the masses under a broader popular suffrage. Let us examine first their imperialism, then their Tory democracy.

Imperialism. June 24, 1872 was the date marking the start of Tory neo-imperialism and the so-called "second British empire." On that day Disraeli delivered a famous speech (*Document 11*) in the Crystal Palace in London, attacking the Liberal party of William Gladstone (1809-1898) for neglecting the empire. During the 1870's, Disraeli made Queen Victoria Empress of India, acquired control of the Suez Canal in Egypt, and expanded imperialism in Africa. In contrast, Burke had fought the excesses of royal British imperialism in both America and India. On such issues Burke, the conservative anti-imperialist Whig, must never be confused with Disraeli and Churchill, the conservative imperialist Tories.

There was an ethical conflict between the increased imperialism and the increased democracy of British Toryism. Its imperialism conflicted with the democratic aspirations of other countries and the awakening of Asia and Africa. British imperialism could still score brilliant successes in the 1870's under Disraeli; Churchill in his youth could still participate in its victorious Boer war in South Africa; Churchill in his old age was forced to witness its total defeat in India, Egypt, Palestine. What then remains today of Disraeli's and Churchill's imperialism? Not their untenable control of colonial peoples and other non-Anglo-Saxons but their tenable ideal of the voluntary unity of Anglo-Saxon dominions with the mother country.

Tory Democracy Plus Monarchism. In order to face the new, post-Burkean conditions of modern industrialism, Disraeli founded "Tory democracy." The term may be defined as the attempt to *root* the new industrial masses in the ancient conservative traditions by welcoming them into parliament and politics. Burke, writing before his aristocracy had lost its social base, made strong speeches against extending the vote. Disraeli in 1867 argued strongly for his bill giving the vote to urban workers. He based his argument not on a radical faith in innovations or a liberal faith in the masses but on the need for providing a broader base for the same old traditions of monarchy, constitution, established church.

Attitudes Toward Change. The ottantottist and the

revolutionary both oppose peaceful change—the former because he opposes change, the latter because the peaceful kind is too slow. But Tory democracy and rationalist liberalism both favor peaceful change—how then do they differ? They differ, wrote Disraeli, by whether they link change with concrete traditions or with abstractions: "In a progressive country change is constant; and the great question is not whether you should resist change which is inevitable but whether that change should be carried out in deference to the manners, the customs, the laws, the traditions of the people or in deference to abstract principle and arbitrary and general doctrines."

Disraeli vs. Peel. By the reform bill of 1832, the Whig party extended the vote to the middle class, who in turn voted Whig thereafter. From that day on, the Tory party faced a crisis: how win future elections now that its landed aristocrats were too few to outvote the enfranchised commercial class? Two solutions were offered. The Tory leader, Sir Robert Peel (1788-1850), advocated broadening the party's base by wooing the middle class away from the Whigs. His young enemy, Disraeli, advocated broadening the base by wooing the workingman. Both men introduced measures for their respective solutions. As Prime Minister in 1846, Peel repealed the Corn Laws. These grain tariffs had protected the Tory landed aristocrats but enraged the Whig middle classes and starved the city folk. By repealing these laws, the humane Peel did win many middle-class voters from the Whigs. But he did so at the cost of splitting the Tory party and of losing his aristocratic supporters to the Disraeli wing of the party. Eventually the Peelite Tories amalgamated with the Whigs to form the new Liberal party under Gladstone.

Social Conscience. The defeat of the Peelite middle-class solution gave Disraeli his chance. The Disraeli solution was to combine both ends against the middle: to ally rural landlords and urban workers against the commercial middle class. That solution enabled the Tory party, thereafter known as the "Conservative" party, to survive the middle-class victories of 1832 and 1846 (the Reform Bill and the end of the Corn Laws) and to make Disraeli prime minister in 1868 and 1874-1880. Sometimes Disraeli's cultivation of the worker is called "Tory socialism." Since the definitions of socialism are endless and since the word is sometimes taken in the left-wing and Marxist sense of class war rather than class alliance, the alternative terms "Tory democracy" and "Tory social conscience" may prove less confusing than "Tory socialism."

The best primary sources for this Tory democracy are the pro-worker speeches and essays found in the Disraeli anthology, *The Radical Tory*, London, 1937, and Disraeli's social novels, *Coningsby,* 1844 and *Sybil,* 1845. The two novels expressed the worker-plus-aristocrat ideals of his "Young England" movement. The subtitle of *Sybil* was "The Two Nations," meaning the rich and the poor. The book denounced middle-class capitalist liberals for condoning "the most miserable tenements in the most hideous borough in the ugliest country in the world." Even Karl Marx (1818-1883) was forced to admit grudgingly the social insight of the Conservative Disraeli. But in contrast with Marx's class war, Disraeli's Tory democracy or "Tory socialism" reconciled "the two nations" by making the party of aristocracy and conservatism take the lead in improving the working conditions of the poor.

Disraeli did not merely give lip service to the workers; he also "delivered the goods." Extending the vote to the urban workers, Disraeli's electoral Reform Bill of 1867 did for them what the Whig Reform Bill of 1832 did for the manufacturers. During his ministry of 1874-1880, Disraeli legalized trade unions, peaceful pickets, and the right to strike. Further, not the Liberals but his Tory party introduced the Employers' and Workman's Act and the Conspiracy Act of 1875. Workers hailed these Acts, which improved working conditions, as "the charter of trade union liberties" for the next twenty-five years. In the words not of a conservative but of a subsequent Labor member of parliament, Alexander Macdonald, "The Conservative party have done more for the working classes in five years than the Liberals have done in fifty."

Here is Disraeli's own definition of Tory democracy: "Instead of falling under . . . the thraldom of capital— under those who, while they boast of their intelligence, are more proud of their wealth—if we must find a new force to maintain the ancient throne and monarchy of England, I, for one, hope that we may find that novel power in the invigorating energies of an educated and enfranchised people." But there are two sides to Tory democracy, the Tory side as well as the democracy side. At the same time as Disraeli urged his party to look forward to "the invigorating energies" of the workers, he urged it to look backward to all those historic traditional institutions into which the new energies must be safely canalized.

Disraeli on the Constitution.   Disraeli shared Burke's emotional veneration for the British constitution but added to it the more philosophical basis of Coleridge. Coleridge taught Disraeli to see the constitution as the organic union of separate classes or "orders," each with special historic loyalties, privileges, duties. This class balance, argued Disraeli and Coleridge, must not be upset by the attempt of the middle class, via the Reform Bill of 1832, to become dictators over the other "orders" behind the facade of democracy. Disraeli elaborated these Coleridgean concepts in his speeches, his novels, and in two key essays: *Vindication of the English Constitution*, 1835; *Letters of Runnymede*, 1836.

Churchill: Evolutionary Reformer.   A nobleman descended from the Duke of Marlborough, young Churchill entered parliament as a Conservative deputy at the age of twenty-five. He continued to be a leading political figure for more than half a century. (*See Document 24.*) Following the Disraeli tradition of his father Randolph, young Winston accused the Conservative party of betraying "Tory democracy" and embracing plutocracy on issues like the tariff. He lamented in 1903: "The old Conservative party with its religious convictions and constitutional principles will disappear and a new party will arise . . . like perhaps the Republican party in the United States of America . . . rigid, materialist and secular, whose opinions will turn on tariffs and who will cause the lobbies to be crowded with the touts of protected industries." This was a typical Disraeli-style speech, in which the young aristocrat sought to revive the alliance between nobles and common people against the alleged plutocrats of big business. Because his party abandoned that alliance, Churchill temporarily joined the Liberal party. There he worked closely with the Liberal orator, David Lloyd George (1863-1945). Together they achieved social reforms, lower tariffs, workers' pensions, improved factory conditions, and other social security measures long before the American New Deal. Churchill's mo-

tive was not "progressive" but conservative: to root
the workers in the traditional framework by showing
them they could satisfy their needs within that framework instead of with Marxist class war.

Churchill's readiness to work temporarily with Liberals in order to make capitalism more humane typifies
the evolutionary as opposed to ottantottist conservative.
The ideal of British statesmen of all parties since 1688
has usually been such a balanced middle-road. Consequently distinctions between Liberal, Conservative, and
Laborite become constantly blurred in this least doctrinaire, least ideological country in the world, a country
where playing by ear is more important than abstract
"systems" of left or right.

Attacks Socialism.   The same Churchill who introduced social reforms during 1906-1912 enraged many
workers by breaking the nationwide "general strike" of
1925. His reply: general strikes are not lawful economic
evolution but lawless political revolution. In his unsuc-
cessful election campaign of 1945 he lost still more votes
by alleging: socialism leads to a police state because it
brings so many bureaucratic controls that "only a Ges-
tapo" can enforce them. Thereupon the "worker's friend"
of 1906 stood accused as the worker's foe of 1945. Indeed, ever since the strike of 1925, he had been charged
with betraying his pre-1914 record as an evolutionary
reformer. The same charge of inconsistency and betrayal
had been made against Burke for opposing France's
revolution after supporting America's. We have seen
the distinction Burke made between the two revolutions
in answering that charge. Churchill similarly distinguished
between helping the worker with concrete social reforms
and arousing him to class war with abstract socialist
ideologies. So Burkean a distinction typifies the British
distrust of abstract messianic blueprints. That distrust
is shared by all classes, notably by the trade-unionist
(non-"Bevanite") wing of the Labor party, a wing often
recognized as "more traditionally British" and more conservative (with a small "c") than many a "titled snob"
of the Conservative party.

Change within Framework.   Many Englishmen view
their politics not as a case of choosing between their
parties—Liberals, Laborites, Conservatives—but of seeing that they alternate in office in a fashion corresponding

with the alternating needs of society. Many British Conservatives admit the need for intervals of Labor party rule. Many British Laborites admit the need for Conservative intervals to consolidate and filter the gains of the preceding Labor intervals. In the opinion of many moderates, the Labor victory of 1945 and the Conservative victory of 1951 supplemented each other as useful halves of the same traditional pattern: namely, change within framework.

Non-Socialist Welfare State.   After World War II, Tory democracy partly became the Tory welfare state. But only in part: equally insistent on the statist menace of socialism and on the need for humane social evolution, the present philosophy of the British Conservative party supports free enterprise in normal situations, state intervention in emergencies. One such emergency was housing. In the election campaign of 1951, the Churchill government promised 300,000 state-built housing units annually for workers. Labor derided the promise as impossible, only to find the Tory government building one million units.

Pros and   Cons of Tory Democracy.   Proponents say: Disraeli and Churchill, by their social-welfare reforms, were assimilating industrialism into traditionalism. They went too far, according to ottantottists; not far enough, according to socialists. Opponents attribute insincerity: a trick to win votes from the left by stealing its platform. Proponents reply: is not that same flexibility the advantage of evolutionary conservatism over the Maistrean kind? British conservatism prides itself on adopting innovations from the left whenever these pass the Burkean test not of theory but of experience.

Opponents point out three undeniable facts: (1) after Disraeli's death and despite him, commercial interests replaced landed aristocracy as the real power in the Conservative party; (2) workers consequently turned first to the Liberals and then to the Laborites; (3) a majority of low-income groups vote anti-Conservative today. Do these three facts not reduce Tory democracy to an empty slogan? Proponents reply: (1) the minority of workers (probably a third) that does still vote Conservative is a large one; (2) it is large enough to prevent the disastrous class war that would result if party lines corresponded entirely with class lines; (3) that large minority of working-class Conservatives would never have existed in the first place—conservatism would have vanished, class war and civil war would wrack England today—if the Tories had followed Peel's wooing of the middle class instead of Disraeli's wooing of the workers; hence the importance of Disraeli's pro-trade-union laws of the 1870's. . . . These allegations of opponents and proponents must be assessed with equal respect; sound authorities are found on both sides.

Cassandra. The epithet "Cassandra," taken from the name of Homer's ignored prophetess of Trojan doom, is today often applied to any unheeded prophet. To no one have contemporary writers applied it more frequently than to Churchill, first with sarcasm, later with awe. During 1918-1920 he warned the world that bolshevism would become a world menace, unless strangled in its cradle by timely aid to the anti-bolshevik, liberty-loving majority of the Russian people. Many "experts" of 1920 declared that Churchill had gone crazy and that bolshevism would soon be forgotten. After 1933, he gave the world his second great warning: that Hitler meant war and that Britain must rearm and support international coöperation against nazi aggression. For the second time he was declared "hysterical." The Conservative government excluded him during the 1930's; it followed Neville Chamberlain, the finance expert from Birmingham, in trying to appease the dictators. According to Churchill supporters, Chamberlain (1869-1940) symbolized the unaristocratic Birmingham spirit of "the man in trade." Although more aware of the Hitler danger, the Labor party likewise persisted in a suicidal disarmament. The discrediting of appeasement by World War II finally enabled Churchill to replace Chamberlain as the Conservative Prime Minister, 1940-1945.

Churchill's third great warning took place in 1946 at Fulton, Missouri. There he told a complacent world that Soviet Russia threatened it with aggressions as dangerous as Hitler's had been. Even Conservative newspapers in Britain and leading right-wing Republican newspapers in America denounced the Fulton speech as "hysterical war-mongering" and as sowing distrust of "our Soviet allies." His defenders have retorted: that speech was the shock that awoke the slumbering West to halt Soviet world conquest in the nick of time. As the subsequent

correctness of his unpopular anti-Hitler warning brought
Churchill to office in 1940, so the subsequent correctness of his unpopular anti-Stalin warning helped elect
him Prime Minister in 1951, avenging his defeat of 1945
by the Labor party. The fourth unpopular warning by
the Cassandra of conservatism occurred in 1954; drama-
tizing for mankind the menace of atomic war, he urged
a peace not of appeasement but of negotiation through
strength. Aged 80 and already proved right only too often
by history, he retired from the premiership voluntarily
in 1955.

III LATIN EUROPE

— 7 —

MAISTRE: CATHOLIC
MONARCHIST

Changing Content of French Conservatism. The
three chapters on French thought deal with three rival
types of conservative: clerical monarchist; moderate evolutionary; nationalist. All three also reflect the changing
sources of power in Europe as a whole: from aristocracy
to upper middle class to masses. The present chapter
centers around Maistre, a monarchist addressing himself
to nobles and clergy. The next chapter concerns Tocqueville and Taine, moderates addressing themselves to the
highly educated upper middle class. The third chapter
on France discusses Barrès and Maurras, nationalists
addressing themselves to the nation as a whole.

Background of Maistre. After the breakdown of
the French Revolution, Count Joseph de Maistre (1753-
1821) became the most influential philosophical spokesman for restoring the old days. (*See Document 8.*)
Against the slogan "liberty, equality, fraternity," he
seemed almost personally to embody the slogan "throne
and altar." His program: a restoration of hereditary
monarchy, only this time more religious, less frivolous
than before. His attitude reflected his biography: a har-

assed refugee, he had to flee from his native Savoy to
escape the invading armies of the French Revolution.
(Savoy then was a French-speaking province of the
Italian-speaking monarchy of Piedmont-Sardinia.) A
nobleman and diplomat, he became for fourteen years
Sardinian ambassador to Russia. His ottantottist faith
was strengthened by seeing absolute monarchy still functioning in Russia as before 1789.

Against "Rights of Man." Liberal critics of the
French Revolution would join Maistre in attacking its
unliberal reign of terror. Where he went far beyond them
was in also attacking two achievements of the Revolution that liberals admired: its listing of universal "Rights
of Man" and its several attempts at a written constitution.
Real constitutions like the British grew organically out
of history over the centuries. They were rooted in hearts,
not handwriting. The use of pure reason to concoct constitutions or universal rights was the fallacy of *a priori*
thinking (defined in Chapter 2). Society was too complex,
consequences too unpredictable, and human reason too
feeble to take the fearful risk of remaking society. Better
leave it alone despite its many faults. Tampering and
"progress" would result not in the intended noble "rights
of man" but in civil war, mass misery, chaos. The foregoing arguments occur in Maistre's *Essay on the Gen-
erative Principle of Political Constitutions,* 1810. He combined (comments John Bowle in *Politics and Opinion*)
"an Augustinian conviction of Original Sin with a Hob-
besian political pessimism."

Pragmatic vs. Divine Sanction.   Both ottantottist and
evolutionary conservatives defend monarchy as a social
cement needed to hold society together, to keep it "organic," not "atomistic." But while the Maistre school
defends monarchy as absolute, the evolutionary British
school defends it merely as "pragmatic"; that is, as useful. For example, during the crisis of 1936 over the
abdication of King Edward VIII, the secretary of conservative Prime Minister Stanley Baldwin wrote (Thomas
Jones, *A Diary with Letters,* London, 1954): "What a
problem the king has been. We invest our rulers with
qualities which they do not possess, and we connive at
the illusion—those of us who know better—because monarchy is an illusion which works. It has a 'pragmatic
sanction.' " But continental monarchists like Maistre

defended monarchy not as a pragmatic illusion but as a divinely sanctioned absolute.

Having postulated an absolute sanction for monarchy, Maistre became slave of his own infallible logic. He carried his logic to the point of demanding "love" even for an "unjust" ruler, earthly or heavenly: "We find ourselves in a realm whose sovereign has proclaimed his laws. . . . Some . . . appear hard and even unjust. . . . What should be done? Leave the realm, perhaps? Impossible: the realm is everywhere. . . . Since we start with the supposition that the master exists and that we must serve him absolutely, is it not better to serve him, whatever his nature, with love than without it?" This Kafka-like chain of reasoning reaches its climax in a logical if inhuman paradox: "The more terrible God appears to us . . . the more our prayers must become ardent. . . ." Cruel as these arguments sound, note that the motive of the personally mild Maistre was humane: revolts against cruel authority would inflict *even* crueler sufferings on mankind. He drew this lesson from the French Revolution: submission to traditional authority, though admittedly a bitter pill, was Europe's cure for its still bitterer chaos.

Clericalism. Even Maistre sometimes scolded abuses in the secular part of the *"ancien régime,"* as Frenchmen called the society before 1789. He was more enthusiastic about defending clerical than secular authority (though defending both). For his politics was a theological drama, in which "order" (his key concept) was angelic, "chaos" diabolic, and "revolution" Original Sin. Seduced by the glittering *Social Contract* of Rousseau, giddy and inexperienced nations might lust after democracy or a plebeian Bonapartist dictatorship. But they would come to a perfectly dreadful end; served them right, too, for provoking the wages of sin: "Because she [*Europe*] is guilty, she suffers" (1810). From suffering she will learn that the purest order is a fatherly Christian monarchy. Even kings must avoid rocking the boat of order with liberal "innovations;" Europe must "suspect" the word "reform" (1810). In *Concerning the Pope* (*Du Pape*, 1817), he analyzed "order" further: its hierarchical pyramid logically required one supreme apex. That apex must be no earthly monarch, of whom there were so many, but the union of earthly and spiritual power in the papacy.

"Pope and Executioner." The vast extent of the instability following the French Revolution surprised even its supporters. How re-stabilize society? According to Maistre's *Evening Conservations in Saint Petersburg* (left unfinished 1821), the solution was more faith and more police. That combination he summed up in his own frank formula: "the Pope and the executioner." The Pope was the positive bulwark of order: he gave faith. The executioner was the negative bulwark: he suppressed disorder. Himself an intellectual, Maistre indicted intellectuals as "rebellious" and "insolent" fomenters of disorder.

Maistre vs. Burke. Burke and Maistre attacked the same foe: a meddling rationalism tampering with traditional roots. Their solutions differed: the British constitution, as the embodiment of concrete experience, versus the Church, as the embodiment of faith. They also differed in how large a degree of absolutism they would defend, the unparliamentary Maistre going much further than the British parliamentarian. Maistre went so far as to defend the Spanish Inquisition. Today ottantottists on the continent—Bourbon and Romanov restorationists, the more extreme papists—descend from Maistre in the same way that evolutionary conservatives in England and America descend from Burke.

Case for Maistre. Maistre's proponents put their case something like this. Burke's cure for social ills, the English Constitution, was suited only to one country, offered little to others. Maistre's cure, Catholic monarchy, was better because more universal, being applicable to all countries. Even though his return to monarchy has become unrealistic, he still performs one outstanding service: he forces progress-minded intellectuals to face up to the horrors of revolution, whether French or Russian. In France, the cult of "the left" and *la grande Révolution* is so deep it forces even an unradical capitalist party like the current "Radical Socialists" to retain a revolutionary-sounding name in order to retain voters. The same myth of revolution that made capitalists call themselves "Radical Socialists" made it difficult after 1945 to rally French intellectuals to defend themselves against communist aggression. They sometimes seem too intoxicated with the slogans of 1789, now parroted by the new aggressor from Russia. To unmask the terrorist reality behind grand democratic slogans (of 1789 or of

1917) remains Maistre's indispensable function in Latin
Europe and Latin America.

Case Against Maistre. Thus his proponents. Meanwhile his opponents fall into two groups: liberals and
Burkean conservatives. Democratic liberals accuse Maistre
of exaggerating the admitted defects of the democratic
awakening of 1789 in order to justify his own outmoded
class of kings, nobles, and priests, parasitic exploiters
of the Common Man. Burkean conservatism accuses
Maistre of resembling the Jacobin rationalists; even
though with opposite premises, they and Maistre both
were abstract, deductive logicians. Burke was concrete
and inductive; he preferred prudence and experience to
deductive logic. In the Burkean sense, not Maistre but
Tocqueville was the true French conservative. To use a
distinction Burke himself might have made: Burke had
less brilliance but more common sense than his abstract
French rivals, whether Maistrean conservatives or Voltairean liberals.

This distinction raises the question: what kind of
personality was Maistre himself? Hasty readers of his
glorification of faith and papacy may guess he was a
priest or in the service of the church or at least was
primarily religious in temperament. Nothing of the sort!
He was a very wordly layman in the service not of the
church but of the Savoy monarchy. By temperament he
was in no way mystical nor even primarily religious but
a dry, nimble logician, educated in the best secular scholarship of the day. He resembled not the church fathers
but the dry, nimble minds of the rationalists he attacked.
He reached his glorification of unreason and of divine
authority not by ecstatic religious mysticism, not by in-
tuition, not even by accepting traditional authority
(though he preached acceptance) but by using his own
mind independently, rationally, and with steps of deductive logic.

Though Maistre would never have admitted it, let us
characterize him as the last and ablest abstract rationalist
of the whole Voltairean Age of Reason. Even more than
the rationalist Voltaire and as much as the rationalist
Jacobins, Maistre believed in pure and absolute ideas; only
his idea was absolute authority rather than absolute
reason. In Maistre the destructive deductive logic of the
eighteenth century got carried so far that it destroyed

even itself, Pure Reason committing suicide for the sake of Pure Order.

Bonald. Maistre's contemporary, the writer Louis de Bonald (1754-1840), was likewise an ottantottist authoritarian. An émigré during the French Revolution, Bonald returned to France in 1806, became minister of instruction under Napoleon, and then an extreme Bourbon royalist under the Bourbon restoration that followed 1815. The names of Maistre and Bonald are closely linked in most studies. In one respect they differed: Maistre went further than Bonald by putting papal above monarchic authority.

Veuillot. The overthrow of the last Bourbon ruler of France in 1830 discredited Maistre's influence for a while. It was reborn in the second half of the nineteenth century after liberal disillusionment with the revolutions of 1848. Louis Veuillot, 1813-1883 (*see Document 20*), was France's most influential disciple of Maistre. He edited the important Catholic newspaper, *L'Univers Religieux* after 1843 and wrote *The Pope and Diplomacy,* 1861, *The Liberal Illusion,* 1866. Like many conservatives who love the past aesthetically (Goethe, Coleridge, Wordsworth, Newman, Keble, Arnold, Poe, Melville), Veuillot, too, published books of poetry. Midcentury French Catholics were split between the Maistre views of *L'Univers Religieux* and the partly liberal and modernist Catholicism represented by Dupanloup, Bishop of Orléans, and Sibour, Archbishop of Paris. Veuillot's side was supported by essays from his friend Cortés, Spanish ambassador to France during 1850-1853. In 1858-1859, Veuillot deepened and strengthened the philosophical roots of French conservatism by editing the French edition of Cortés' works.

Pius IX. Finally Pius IX, Pope during 1846-1878 and a disillusioned exliberal, decided the controversy in favor of the Veuillot side. Pius did this by publishing a papal encyclical, *The Syllabus of Errors,* 1864. (*See Document 19.*) It was the greatest international triumph ever achieved by the Maistre-style conservatives. For millions of Catholics all over the world, it listed and condemned the assumptions of liberalism, rationalism, secularism, and scientific scepticism. It was a public rebuke to those more moderate French Catholics (liberals and evolutionary conservatives) whose newspaper, the *Corre-*

spondant, had attacked the Maistre-Cortés views of Veuillot's *L'Univers.* Aside from its important theology, the *Syllabus* of 1864, reinforced by the dogma of papal infallibility in 1870, caused a political earthquake. It caused a renewed war to the hilt between French Catholicism and French republicanism. Later, that war was partly overcome by the more conciliatory Pope Leo XIII, elected 1878, and his more conciliatory encyclical, *Rerum Novarum,* 1891. *Rerum Novarum* founded the more open-minded outlook toward social questions of two great modern Catholic leaders of evolutionary conservatism: De Gasperi of the Italian Christian Democratic party, and Adenauer of the German Christian Democratic party.

Other Maistre Influences. Maistre's stress on the need for the individual to submit to society influenced nonclerical and even anti-clerical figures, including socialists. That aspect of Maistre was given a more left-wing application by Count Claude de Saint-Simon (1760-1825), founder of French utopian socialism. Napoleon III, Emperor of the French 1852-1870, adopted some of Maistre's statism through reading Saint-Simon. So did Auguste Comte (1798-1857), founder of French "positivism," a nonclerical materialist who hailed scientists as the priests of the future. Among the great French novelists, Honoré Balzac (1799-1850) most showed Maistre's influence, though indirectly. Balzac sympathized with the old aristocracy. He satirized as vulgar the new, commercial middle class. The Maistre influence seems apparent in Balzac's novel *Père Goriot,* 1834, and in his anti-liberal, even reactionary "Foreword" to *La Maison Du Chat Qui Pelotte,* 1830. In twentieth-century France, Maistre's influence was felt by the nonclerical sociologist Emile Durkheim (1858-1917) and the "Catholic atheist," Charles Maurras. France's great religious poet Paul Claudel (1868-1955) expressed Maistre's influence at a more sensitive, spiritual level.

— 8 (Latin Europe) —

TOCQUEVILLE AND TAINE: MODERATE ANTI-JACOBINS

Tocqueville's Writings. Count Alexis de Tocqueville, 1805-1859, lived like a French version of an English country gentleman. He spent most of his life in shy—or haughty—retirement; he himself called it "morose isolation." An exception was his brief public service of 1848-1852 under the Second French Republic. His scathing *Reflections* (*Souvenirs*) about this experience were published posthumously, 1893. His best known books were *Democracy in America,* 1835-1838, and twenty years later *Ancien Régime and the Revolution.*

He was deeply influenced by British liberals as well as by conservative anti-revolutionaries of the continent. Some excellent authorities call him liberal; some, conservative. Liberal was his open-minded approach and his criticism of Bourbon monarchy and the days before 1789. Conservative was his warning that democratic conformity may stifle liberty and that equality and liberty are opposites, not synonyms. His mind was totally independent. Its lonely truths upset liberal and conservative clichés equally. Today many readers find his insights more original and exciting than ever. (*See Document 12.*)

America. Tocqueville's *Democracy in America* has been called the profoundest book ever written about our country. He found more to praise than to blame in our democratic experiment. But by predicting with uncanny accuracy the nature of our future demagogues and thought-controllers, he warned America against the intolerance, the stifling conformity of mob pressure. So doing, he took the characteristically conservative stand that equality threatens liberty: "Americans are so enamored of equality they would rather be equal in slavery than unequal in freedom." But our severest critic was also our warmest friend: "The principal instrument of America is freedom; of Russia, slavery."

Direct Elections: Unheeded Warning. Factors making Tocqueville slightly more conservative than liberal were his aristocratic distrust of the common people and of direct democracy. He expressed this distrust in political action by his role as a government official during the revolution of 1848. A committee of the French National Assembly was drawing up a new constitution to serve the newly proclaimed Second Republic. He warned it against its project for direct election of a president by universal suffrage. He predicted that this method of election would produce not liberty but dictatorship, masked in democratic trappings. Indirectly influenced perhaps by Rousseau's cult of the "General Will" of the masses and by liberal faith in the goodness of man, the Assembly ignored the warning of its great historian-prophet. The result, at the close of 1848, was the direct election of Louis Napoleon as president via universal suffrage, followed later by his forcible suppression of civil liberties and his election as Emperor Napoleon III, based on mass plebiscites. Had there been indirect election of presidents via the French Assembly, thus putting liberty ahead of equality, then the despotism-plotting nephew of the first Napoleon could never have been elected, according to Tocquevillean reasoning.

In 1933 the nazis further fulfilled Tocqueville's warning that equal electoral rights may lead to the extinction of rights and that the winning of democratic elections may be the end of elections and the suicide of democracy. In his prophecy of dictatorship-by-plebiscite as a democratic mask for tyranny, Tocqueville anticipated the nazis and the Soviet "People's Democracies." Both those modern totalitarians use democratic plebiscites based on universal suffrage. That is why Tocqueville's distrust of direct democracy and plebiscites has received more recognition today than in the nineteenth century.

"Recollections." Tocqueville's eye-witness *Recollections* of the Revolution of 1848 contained three assumptions fundamental to conservatism: protection of a traditional framework, rejection of majority dictatorship, and rejection of *a priori* blueprints of socialist utopia. Of his own governmental role, he wrote: "my only aim" was "to protect the ancient laws of society against the innovators" and "to cause the evident will of the French people to triumph over the passions and desires of the

Paris workman," in other words, "to conquer demagogism by democracy." By democracy he meant not majority
dictatorship but a majority rule sternly limited by morality. In contrast with Maistre and the royalists, Tocqueville
recognized the inevitability of constant change. In contrast with liberal relativists, he urged a permanent framework of what he called "forms": to canalize the inevitable
change. Hence, he fought his socialist and radical opponents not with the fanatic authoritarian methods to
which the monarchist camp had by then degenerated but,
to repeat his own significant words, "with democracy."

Against Abstractions. Like British conservatives
and unlike many French ones, Tocqueville defended the
concrete reality against the promises of *a priori* theory.
For example: "The Republic . . . promised more but
gave less liberty than the Constitutional Monarchy."
Being anti-reactionary, he added: he would support the
French Republic anyhow, now that it was there, and
would try to make it work. That seemed to him better
for stability than becoming a counter-revolutionary,
yearning for a monarchy too long uprooted to evoke
loyalty.

Tocqueville was sceptical of what he called "general
ideas" and "absolute systems." He looked at the historical
root of things, the relationship of concrete to concrete,
not the piling up of abstraction on abstraction. His writings were one long war against unhistorical and rootless
thinking. He found such thinking, on the one hand,
among liberals, socialists, utopians. He found it, on the
other hand, in the suicidal would-be conservatism of
authoritarians and belated monarchists; their historical
roots were no longer solidly anchored in French soil.
Unlike Maistre, Tocqueville concluded that, once a monarchy has permanently lost its historical roots, a traditionalist is no longer obligated to defend it.

Not merely his balanced politics but his psychological
insight has caused contemporary new conservatives to
rediscover Tocqueville. He is perhaps the favorite conservative writer in what may be called, without sarcasm,
the world of literary intellectuals. Many consider him the
most perceptive blender of the best of liberalism with the
best of conservatism. His wisdom stood for evolutionary
change within—not without—lasting "forms."

Taine. Conservatism has been called the rebuttal

to the French Revolution. The history of the Revolution by the great historian Hippolyte Taine (1828-1893) is often considered the most mature of these rebuttals, the most balanced, the most steeped in its subject. Despite other differences, Taine's moderate kind of anti-Jacobin conservatism was closer to Tocqueville's than to the extremer kinds, such as clerical monarchism or authoritarian nationalism. Taine, too, discarded the monarchist nostalgia of the Maistre-Veuillot school of anti-Jacobins. A conservative outlook is often the result of having witnessed personally an unbearable degree of revolutionary disorder. Examples are Burke, Coleridge, Maistre, Metternich. In the case of Taine, there were two upsetting personal experiences of disorder in the France of 1870-1871: the disintegration of the Second Empire; the civil war inaugurating the Third Republic. The books composing Taine's *Origines de la France Contemporaine* were *Ancien Régime,* 1876; *Révolution,* 1878-1884; *Régime Moderne,* 1890. Their themes included contempt for Bonapartism, for revolutionary change, for the masses, and for optimistic illusions about progress or equality.

Against Centralizing. Taine offended all parties of France simultaneously. He simultaneously condemned— for the same centralizing tendency—the Bourbon monarchy, the French Revolution, the Bonapartist dictatorship, and the centralizing republicans of his own day. Their shared centralization replaced the traditional provincial decentralization of an older France. Thereby they crushed that spirit of local independence, those rich and rooted variations which conservatives cherish. Those precious diversities, evolved organically out of history, are defended by such traditionalists against liberal as well as reactionary centralizers. Taine's most conservative achievement was to demonstrate that most French republicans and liberals, though claiming to be the opposite of the old Bourbon regime, actually shared its worst defect: a fanatic mania for centralization, smothering liberty, individuality, and French traditionalism. Distrusting slogans and grand abstractions, whether republican or royalist, Taine tried to explain them in terms of three concrete things: national background (so-called race), epoch, and surroundings. Like Tocqueville, he tried to see ideas in their concrete historical context.

BARRÈS AND MAURRAS: AUTHOR-ITARIAN NATIONALISTS

Against Rootlessness. The French novelist and political philosopher, Maurice Barrès (1862-1923), was both conservative and nationalist. He represented the area where these two separate movements overlapped. That area was their shared loathing for rootlessness. Thus *The Uprooted* (*Les Déracinés,* 1897) was the title of one of his most influential novels.

Sacrificing Individual to Nation. Barrès was born in Lorraine, a border province taken by France from Germany in 1871. Already as a boy, he helped Lorraine resist Germanization. No wonder his French nationalism became emotional, aggressive. According to his novels, essays, and bristling manifestos, everything, including life and liberty, must be sacrificed to the nation-state, if necessary. Individual freedom must be subordinated entirely to the collective freedom of the nation. French national characteristics must be kept undefiled, mixed marriages discouraged. As a young newspaper correspondent, he attended the Dreyfus trial in 1899; he violently opposed Captain Dreyfus, an innocent scapegoat framed as a spy by anti-Semitic French army officers. The Barrès philosophy rated the collective national prestige of the French army above justice to a mere individual.

"Integral Nationalism." The collective "national soul" was a favorite concept of Barrès and his disciples. Partly it merely reflected the conservative preference for organic over atomistic societies. But Barrès carried it to a new extreme. Earlier supporters of organic society like Maistre wanted it static and calm; Barrès wanted it more dynamic with "energy," another key concept. Thus the subtitle of *The Uprooted* was "a novel of national energy." Earlier conservatives, even the internationalists, had revered nationality also: as a social cement. But with Barrès we enter "integral nationalism," a nationalism unqualified and all-embracing. Earlier traditionalists conserved many different historical roots; Barrès conserved only one. This narrowed conservatism was the core of his speech of 1916 (*See Document 26*), glorifying "holy war" for the fatherland. That sentiment was found in all countries after 1870. Though also authoritarian, a Maistre, however, could never be a narrow nationalist, never a racist. Maistre had been an international Christian conservative in the cosmopolitan spirit of Metternich's Congress of Vienna.

Hero Worship. Like Carlyle in England and the romantic school in Germany, Barrès tried to popularize the cult of the hero. His cult, like theirs, lacked ethical discrimination; it minimized his heroes' crimes. It also lacked ideological discrimination; he worshipped all "exceptional men," to cite his phrase, regardless of their ideologies. He praised the Bourbon kings, the anti-Bourbon Napoleon, and even liberals like Ernest Rénan (1823-1890) so long as they seemed "heroic." Hero worship led Barrès to support the would-be dictatorship of General Boulanger in 1888 and the anti-Semitic "League of Patriots" of Paul Déroulède (1846-1914). But during World War I, Barrès publicly repudiated his former anti-Semitism of the Dreyfus days and now declared French culture open to all races alike. A transitional figure, Barrès was still too conservative, too devoted to traditional institutions, to replace them with totalitarianism or to carry his blood-cult as far as fascism.

Maurras. It remained for the French author and editor, Charles Maurras (1868-1952), to take the final step from integral nationalism to fascism. Maurras hailed "the music of the prose of Barrès," whose disciple he was partly but not wholly. Maurras hated democracy as decadent and corrupt, loved the glories of French monarchy before 1789, and added to this love the passionate, intolerant nationalism of the Barrès school. Maurras began as a non-fascist, blending the Barrès and Maistre brands of conservatism. He ended as a supporter of French fascism and nazi anti-Semitism. The Fourth Republic tried and convicted him for collaborating with the nazi occupation during World War II. It was ironic that the pupil of Barrès ended by collaborating with the nation Barrès hated most. Yet Maurras was no crude storm-trooper. He was one of the most gifted literary

figures of his day. Even his enemies admired the prose
style of his newspaper, the partly royalist, partly fascist
Action Française. For his literary gifts, he was elected
to the "immortals" of the French Academy.

"Reactionary" vs. "Fascist." Even before Maurras
reached his pro-nazi stage, even while merely a traditional monarchist, his plebiscitarian stress on mass meetings, mass agitation, and mass nationalism was more
fascist than conservative in spirit. To be sure, he praised
with nostalgia the *ancien régime* of the Bourbons and the
papacy. He called himself a royalist and a Catholic (actually a Catholic atheist, for which he was finally excom-
municated by the Pope). But a real conservative, whether
ottantottist or Burkean, distrusts appeals to the masses
and prefers to work through an orderly and lawful aristocratic traditionalism. When Maurras turned to disorderly,
lawless mobs to bring his movement to power, he parted
company even with reactionary conservatism, even with
the Maistre he claimed to admire, and became a fascist.
The counter-revolutionary reaction of a Maistre or a
Pobiedonostsev remains merely reactionary and not fascist
until the turning-point when it seeks its main support no
longer from a traditional (and hence at least partly
ethical) aristocracy but from nationalist lynch-mobs. That
turning-point separated Barrès from Maurras. It still
separates both conservatism and ordinary nationalism
from fascism. Though less sincerely and for other purposes, the fascist radicals of the right are as eager as any
Tom Paine democrat to use mass meetings and "direct
democracy."

Contrast the pro-nazi conservatism or pseudo-conserv-
atism of Maurras in World War II with the anti-nazi
conservatism of Churchill in the same war. The contrast
shows the political consequences of whether or not conservatism sacrifices its means to its ends. All over the
globe, fascist nationalists on the far right tend to make
the same sacrifice of means to ends that communists
make on the far left. Authentic conservatives and liberals
support, while fascists and communists reject, the self-
restraint known as the Christian ethic.

SPAIN: DONOSO CORTÉS

Biography. Ever since Spain's popular resistance to the armies of Napoleon and his new middle-class dispensation, Spain has often been the stubbornest stronghold of the most anti-liberal, anti-modern, anti-democratic ideas and forces in Europe. Juan Donoso Cortés, Marqués de Valdegamas, 1809-1853, hereafter called "Cortés" for brevity, was Spain's ablest representative of philosophical conservatism. In some ways he remains the subtlest intellect in the entire history of conservatism.

Like John Stuart Mill, he was a child prodigy. Cortés may be called the child prodigy of conservatism as Mill was of liberalism. An aristocrat descended from the conqueror of Mexico, he was well educated at the best Spanish schools and universities. He became one of Europe's leading scholars, literary artists, and diplomats. In temperament he remained a philosopher to the end, not a practical politician. Yet his influence on practical politics was considerable, owing to his private influence on royalty. In his youth he shared with most intellectuals the beliefs of eighteenth-century rationalism. In 1830 at Madrid, he was still an optimistic liberal, not yet entirely convinced that human nature ruled out rapid social progress. But he became increasingly disillusioned by the disorder allegedly brought by liberal "French ideas" and their Spanish imitators.

Cortés served in the Ministry of the Interior under Ferdinand VII, who died in 1833, and was elected to the Spanish Parliament from Cadiz in 1837. He tutored Ferdinand's daughter, who later became Queen Isabella II. He was rewarded by being made a member of the Senate. There he championed the rights of throne and altar. But he also stressed that Monarchy must be tempered by religion, mercy, and respect for law. From 1850 until his death in 1853, he was Spanish Ambassador to Paris. His personal acquaintances included his admirer Metternich, Premier Guizot, Napoleon III, and other rulers.

Writings.   Politics aside, Cortés' prose is considered a major artistic achievement. The *Encyclopedia Britannica* (13th edition) called it "the finest specimen of impassioned prose published in Spain during the nineteenth century." Orestes Brownson, American political philosopher, described it as "the most eloquent" he ever read. The chief literary weakness of Cortés was his self-intoxication with rhetoric and paradox. His collected works were published in five volumes in Madrid, 1854-1855. His two most important essays were: *"Memoria sobre la situacion actual de la Monarquia,"* 1832 and *"Ensayo sobre el catolicismo, el liberalismo y el socialismo,"* 1851. The second had the greatest international influence of any nineteenth-century political philosophy by any Spaniard (*see Document 15*). The two essays partly contradict each other. They represent, respectively, an evolutionary and a partly ottantottist conservatism.

Middle-road Essay of 1832.   Cortés' essay of 1832, rightly known as "liberal-conservative," made him nationally famous overnight. It upheld moderate constitutional modernism. It condemned both Jacobin and Carlist extremists. Carlism was named after King Ferdinand's younger brother; Carlos disputed the throne with Ferdinand's daughter and chosen successor, Isabella. The medieval absolutists (ottantottists) rallied to Carlos. The constitutionalists (liberals and moderate conservatives), including Cortés, rallied to the infant Isabella. Just as Metternich had called French Royalists "white Jacobins," so Cortés condemned Carlists for being radicals of the right. Still optimistic about achieving a middle road, the Cortés position of 1832 resembled the evolutionary conservatism of Tocqueville in France. Like Tocqueville, Cortés wanted to rebuild the old traditions on the new and educated middle class rather than either the uneducated masses or the medieval lords.

Pessimistic Essay of 1851.   After the European revolutions of 1848, Cortés moved much further toward the authoritarian right than Tocqueville and also further toward clericalism. This change may be attributed to his disillusionment with the fate of middle-roaders in 1848 as well as to his friendship since 1849 with Veuillot, French disciple of Maistre. Pope Pius IX greatly admired the 1851 essay, sent Cortés a papal blessing for it, and incorporated some of its anti-liberal positions into the

Syllabus of Errors. In contrast with 1832, the essay of 1851 no longer represented a synthesis between conservatism and liberalism but a choice. It defined liberals as wavering sceptics, socialists as revolutionary materialists. (Both definitions are subject to challenge.) He preferred socialists to liberals for at least having dogmas, though wrong ones. He warned liberals they would be crushed between the millstones of revolutionary socialism and Christian conservatism and must choose one or the other to survive. Today that either-or keeps reappearing in ever new guises; it excludes middle-road compromises. Backed by Pope Pius, it was rejected by liberal Catholics like Lord Acton (1834-1902) in England and Charles de Montalembert (1810-1870) in France.

Cortés was not against reason and freedom. He called reason the legitimate form of political government and respected the role of free will. But these blessings of reason and freedom were limited by man's imperfect nature. Attempts by liberals, democrats, and socialists to exceed those limits ignored the inherently irrational and evil side of man. Such attempts must inherently fail and leave chaos. Yet above the chaos and outliving man's rebellions against authority, the secret conservative pattern of God's law remained written across the eternal stars. On that exalted note ended the essay of 1851.

"Self-worshipping" Man. Different conservatives have different terms for the liberal who rejects the traditional wisdom of the past as an impediment to reason and progress. What Metternich had called "the presumptuous man," the Cortés essay called the "self-worshipping" man. Such a man presumes to remake so complicated a mechanism as human society. This over-simplifying blindness (to the complicatedness of a society evolved by centuries) was the liberal error of 1789 and 1848, according to Metternich and Cortés. Allied with that error, added Cortés, was the liberal and socialist fallacy of seeing evil in political institutions, instead of in the heart of man. If evil is in superficial external institutions, then it can be easily eliminated by rational blueprints. But if evil is innate in human frailty itself, then no changes of political or economic institutions can ever eliminate it. If man and society are so fallible and can never be perfected, concluded his essay of 1851, then religious improvement within the soul matters more than

social and liberal reforms of society. Since the alternative
to the liberal "self-worshipping man" was God-worship
rather than king-worship, Cortés (like Maistre) put religious authority even higher than secular authority.

Four Famous Speeches. During 1832-1853, Cortés'
influential speeches ran a gamut from liberalism to conservatism to semi-authoritarianism. On the whole, they
place him to the right of Burke, to the left of Maistre;
let us consider four examples. In a speech of 1835,
Cortés upheld the need for a party system, elective and
parliamentary, to advise the king and to debate national
problems. But like Burke, he wanted these parliamentary
elections based not on universal suffrage but on a suffrage limited to "the intelligent" and "the best." Cortés
preferred such an aristocracy of intellect to the social
aristocracy. In a speech of 1844, he accused the latter of
centuries of disloyalty to the throne; many, indeed, were
Carlists in the Civil War against his queen. The Spanish
soul he defined as "monarchist," "Catholic," and even
"democratic" (in the sense of popular roots) but not
"aristocratic." He belonged to the monarchist but anti-
Carlist party known as the *moderados.* In a third speech
(January 15, 1845) he urged his party to borrow from
the liberals the principle of free debate as "the life-
principle of all free peoples."

Fourthly we come to his speech of 1849 on dictatorship. It is often quoted out of context by right-wing
extremists as defending dictatorship in general. But he
was defending dictatorship merely as an emergency and
merely when no free alternative remained. Between constitutional liberty and dictatorship, he argued, we must
always choose liberty. But when the only choice was between "dictatorship by insurrection" and "dictatorship
by government," then he did support the latter. Thus his
defense of dictatorship was qualified and secondary. His
primary ideal throughout was an extremely strong yet
constitutional monarchy. Unlike Carlists and Maistre,
the monarchism of Cortés was never absolute. Unlike
them, he declared himself against "divine right" of kings.
Representing the latest scholarship on Cortés, J. P.
Mayer in *Dublin Review* (first quarter, 1951) aptly characterized him in spirit as "a contemporary of Burckhardt, Kierkegaard, and Tocqueville; he is not a 'conservative' thinker like Maistre: he looks, like these great

contemporaries of his, toward the future." The new research of J. J. Kennedy (*Review of Politics,* October, 1952) likewise reverses the old view (similar to the "old view" about Metternich) that Cortés was merely a reactionary bigot.

Choice Between Two Brands of Authoritarianism. To understand his semi-authoritarian viewpoint of 1849-1853 (his speech of 1849, his essay of 1851), we must consider the historical context north of the Pyrenees. In 1848 the French masses overthrew by force the middle-road monarchy of Louis-Philippe. Cortés interpreted this event as invalidating his earlier middle-road hopes: "The monarchy of the divine right of kings came to an end with Louis XVI on the scaffold; the monarchy of glory, with Napoleon on an island; . . . with Louis-Philippe came to an end the last of all possible monarchies, that of prudence." The choice would now be between two kinds of authoritarianism, from below or from above, both evil but the latter a lesser evil because more capable of being balanced.

Politics Unchecked by Tradition Means Despotism. By replacing religious and traditional authority with mass authority, liberals and democrats believed they were increasing human freedom; that, indeed, has always been their most attractive claim, whether in 1789 or today. During 1849-1853, Cortés met that claim head-on by speeches and essays making the following counter-claim: their ending of religious and traditional checks would leave political power unchecked for the first time in history and would thereby produce, out of liberal democracy, not freedom but "the most gigantic and destructive despotism ever known." The emergence of Lenin and Hitler partly proved right that prediction of Cortés, making it one of the most important perceptions in the entire history of conservative thought.

Misused by Fascists. In the twentieth century the German political theorist, Carl Schmitt (see page 83) used these predictions of Cortés in a clever attempt to justify the nazi dictatorship, hailing with joy the doom of liberty that Cortés had predicted with sorrow. But what Cortés detested in democracy, liberalism, and socialism was precisely that unleashing of politics (from religious and traditional controls) which fascism also represents. Fascism is a secular, rootless, and plebeian dictatorship. Hence, its power rages unlimited; it lacks those ethical restraints of church and of tradition on which religious semi-authoritarians like Cortés insisted.

Yet fascist apologists like Schmitt (or in Italy, Giovanni Gentile, 1875-1944) have often been able to misapply such conservative teachings with undeniable effectiveness. That misapplication indicates some inherent weakness in conservatism as a whole, in the opinion of anti-conservatives. In the opinion of conservatives, their philosophers are not to blame for subsequent misuse.

Reconciling His Viewpoints. Are Cortés' pre- and post-1848 viewpoints irreconcilable? Not if seen in two different contexts. England, America, Scandinavia, and Switzerland have organically evolved a special context, in which mass participation in government has unique historical roots. Those roots give their democracy a stability it lacks in the rest of the world. To them the evolutionary, constitutional viewpoint of his 1832 essay would apply. To countries lacking the possibility of a stable kind of democracy or a middle-road kind of parliament, his viewpoint of 1849-1853 would seem more relevant perhaps.

Against "The Rich." An aspect of Cortés almost entirely ignored by contemporary scholars is his conservative anti-plutocracy. Like his Austrian admirer, the "conservative socialist" Metternich, Cortés believed monarchy had the duty of social paternalism. In a brutally frank letter of 1851 to his friend, Queen Isabella's mother, Cortés said the rich had betrayed their Christian duty of charity to the poor. He predicted social revolution unless the united Christian monarchs of Europe started a new epoch of social ethics by helping the poor, curtailing the rich: "Today the only question is of distributing adequately the wealth which is being badly distributed. . . . If the rulers of nations do not resolve it, socialism will come to resolve the problem. . . ."

Significance Today. Cortés' assumption that reason is frail and progress vain can be better understood today, at a time of growing disillusionment with progress, than in the optimistic Victorian age. For that age, he was almost unique in his prophetic forebodings amid smug prosperity. In Europe today, his essay of 1851 still remains one of the most important intellectual weapons against the left. In America, its out-of-print edition of 1925,

SI 7/11

Author:
(Full Name)   Viereck, Peter

Title: Conservatism

Place: Princeton   Publisher: D Van Nostrand

Date: NJ   Edition:

Series: 1956

Subscriber No.	Name of subscriber	Variation in edition	Order to be held	Number of cards wanted

61–1 (rev. 6-66)   (*Stamp on line*)

☆ GPO : 1966—O–220–725

with the imprimatur of Cardinal Hayes, aroused only brief interest among Catholics, none among Protestants. Yet the gloomy Cortés analysis of human nature and of Original Sin seems particularly close to the present American Protestant school of Reinhold Niebuhr. So far, the current rediscovery of Maistre and Burke by American conservatives has ignored Cortés. Yet connoisseurs of his work may find therein a greater literary distinction than Maistre, a greater visionary intensity than Burke or Metternich. Perhaps Cortés best conveys the shattering insight of all of them into the spiritual and cultural price of progress. Modern readers may apply that insight to the human condition without feeling bound to accept its reactionary application to politics. Some may find in that moral questioning of material progress the needed corrective for a country of unhappy and untragic pleasure-seekers.

IV   EAST OF THE RHINE

— 11 —

METTERNICH: INTERNATIONALIST AND "CONSERVATIVE SOCIALIST"

Career. A "Frenchified" German dandy from the Rhineland, witty, pleasure-loving, and arrogant, Clemens von Metternich (1773-1859) entered the Hapsburg diplomatic service at the age of 22. The young nobleman came as a refugee from the invading armies of the French Revolution. Cosmopolitanism and fear of revolution: such were the two decisive biographical facts of this internationalist anti-Jacobin. The Hapsburg empire—its capital Vienna, its ruler Emperor Francis (1768-1835)—centered in Austria and ruled Hungary, Bohemia, and (after 1815) Northern Italy. Thus it, too, was cosmopolitan; nationalism would disrupt it. During 1815-1848 Metternich was its Foreign Minister, part of the time also its Chancellor, and the dominant figure in German and Slavic Central Europe; those three decades are called Europe's "Metternich era." In 1848 he and his aristocratic internationalism were overthrown by the liberal, nationalist, and middle-class revolutions sweeping Europe. The primary sources for studying his ideas are his many memoirs and letters and those of his associates. (*See Document 10.*) The most documented secondary source is Srbik's *Metternich,* Munich, 1925.

Burke and Maistre Influences. The reader will find both Maistrean and Burkean influences in Metternich's "Confession of Faith" (sent to Tsar Alexander I in 1820). Maistrean: "The people know what is the happiest thing for them: namely, to be able to count on the morrow" (an authoritarian remark ignoring liberty). Burkean: "Stability is not immobility." Again Burkean: the ranking of "experience" over "phrases and theories." Both Maistrean and Burkean: ". . . Progress having been accelerated more rapidly than the growth of wisdom . . . experience has no value for the presumptuous man; faith is nothing to him. . . . Laws have no value for him, because he has not contributed to make them." Coleridgean (though only by coincidence): "It is primarily the middle class of society which this moral gangrene [*the presumptuous man*] has affected."

Burkean Arguments Against Liberals. Coining for himself the phrase *"tout à terre, tout historique,"* Metternich accused the liberal revolutions of the 1820's and 1830's in Italy, Spain, and Germany of being unhistorical and unrealistic. They were trying to transplant (from England) free institutions without historic roots on the Continent. He retorted with Burkean arguments about the need for old roots and orderly organic development. Hence, his sarcastic comments on the liberal revolutions in Naples and elsewhere: "A people who can neither read nor write, whose last word is the dagger—fine material for constitutional principles! . . . The English Constitution is the work of centuries. . . . There is no universal recipe for constitutions." Yet his attitude was not always so entirely negative. Just before his fall in 1848, he was at last winning acceptance from the archdukes for his ancient plan of convoking delegates from all the provincial estates to a representative body in Vienna. It was too late.

Old and New View. Historians differ between an

old and new view of Metternich. A majority prefer the
old view, seeing him as almost the worst reactionary
in history. The old view spotlights his Carlsbad decrees
of censorship, 1819. That these decrees inexcusably har-
assed free opinion is undeniable. Indeed, the new view
does not deny his ottantottist aspects. But it stresses, perhaps too far, his evolutionary aspects, hitherto overlooked.
Even so, the Metternich era was obviously more stagnant
in spirit than other eras. His defense: a war-wracked
Europe "needs repose." (Fuller discussion of new vs. old
view: in P. Viereck, *Conservatism Revisited,* New York,
1949.)

Emperor Blocks Reform. Some authorities prefer
to call the repressive side of the so-called "Metternich
system" the "Emperor Francis system." Metternich dominated his emperor in foreign policy, not in Austrian
police administration. Liberals blame Metternich for not
halting the snoopings of the Imperial police—Metternich
who vainly ordered the police to stop opening the mail
of his closest collaborator, Friedrich Gentz. Metternich
urged Francis to introduce more enlightened constitutional reforms and an embryonic parliamentary representation; to reduce censorship in Austria; to stop viola-
tions of Hungary's constitutional rights; to grant Italians
and Slavs partial self-government, with officials of their
own nationality, so as to avoid provoking a nationalist
reaction; in short, to found an evolutionary conservatism
reconciling, in his own significant words of 1832, the
"opposition between the monarchist principles and the
democratic." The ottantottist Francis vetoed the above
demands, demands of which Metternich's liberal foes
could not know at the time. No wonder Metternich
finally made this startling admission: "I am always considered the rock of order, the obstacle to revolution and
warlike enterprise, but I confess to you my innermost
and secret thought is that old Europe and its form of
government are doomed."

Congress of Vienna. Metternich was host and pre-
siding officer of the Congress of Vienna, the international
peace conference of 1815 after the Napoleonic wars.
The Vienna peace was based on certain principles shared
by the Austrian delegate Metternich, the British delegate
Robert Castlereagh (1769-1822), the French delegate
Charles Talleyrand (1754-1838), the ex-liberal Russian

Tsar Alexander I (1777-1825). These principles were conservatism—in reaction against revolutionary France; tradtionalism—in reaction against twenty-five years of rapid change; legitimism—the principle of hereditary monarchy as the only lawful rule; restoration—the ottantottist principle of bringing back the kings ousted after 1789; peace—in reaction against the Napoleonic wars; the enforcement of peace—by subsequent conferences between kings.

Those subsequent conferences of the 1820's were called "the era of congresses" or "the concert of Europe." Their unity, an international trade union of kings, was popularly (and sometimes sarcastically) called the "Holy Alliance," after Tsar Alexander's manifesto of 1815 for an alliance of all Christian rulers. As liberal democrats correctly pointed out, the weakness of that first successful attempt at a "United Nations" was its narrowly aristocratic base. But it did achieve the positive function—and important precedent—of peacefully arbitrating most disputes. Its negative function was the suppression of nationalist and liberal revolutions in Italy, Spain, Germany. During 1815-1848 not only Jacobinism and republicanism but nationalism was revolutionary. Metternich and Talleyrand defined nationalism as mere "national Jacobinism." The Metternich era regarded nationalism somewhat as the West today regards communism.

The debit of the conservative "concert of Europe" was its bigoted suppression of democratic social progress. The credit was its creation of the longest unbroken peace since the Antonine emperors of second-century Rome. During the whole century between 1815 and 1914, there were no world wars. Until the Crimean war of 1854-1856, there were not even local wars between the signatories of Vienna. Castlereagh, whom Metternich called his "alter ego," spoke for all these war-loathing conservatives when he urged at Vienna: "bring the world back to peaceful habits." In contrast with the nationalists of the Great Reversal, Metternich declared: "I have taken Europe as my fatherland."

"Vive La Force" vs. "Old Principles." "What will our friend Metternich say of this great triumph?" asked Nesselrode, the Russian Foreign Minister, in 1827. He was commenting on the victory of Navarino Bay, where the Turks were defeated by a treacherous surprise attack;

METTERNICH 73

and he answered his own question as follows: "He will repeat his old, tiresome principles; he will talk of right; —*vive la force!* It is might which rules the world nowadays, and I am very glad to find that I and my comrades can leave the regulating of affairs to the admirals. These are men to cut the matter short! Never has there been glory comparable to this moment!" In the opinion of those who regard Hitlerism and Stalinism as the logical outgrowth of such militarist power-politics, Metternich reached his greatest stature in his calm comment on Nesselrode's gloating: "This," said Metternich, "is how [*the Jacobins*] Carnot and Danton . . . thought and spoke. They were signally overthrown, however, by the same old and tiresome principles." These two conflicting quotations illuminate the issue between the "old principles" of peace-loving internationalism and the new nationalist *"vive la force!"* (long live force).

"Iron and Blood" vs. "Tables with Green Covers." "Not by speeches and majority votes are the great questions of the day decided . . . but by iron and blood:" —this phrase of Bismarck's of 1862 reflected a political universe incompatible with that reflected by Metternich's remark of 1821: "Is there anything in the world today which can take the place of ink, pens, a conference table with its green cover, and a few greater or smaller bunglers?" Metternich's aristocratic system depended on diplomacy. Democratic liberalism depended on what Bismarck dismissed as "majority votes." Both systems preferred "conference tables" to "iron," "speeches" to "blood." Both sought to internationalize Europe. Both failed because of the civil war between them. The men of words in 1848, both the democrats and the aristocratic diplomats, were replaced by the men of action of 1870, whose *"vive la force!"* helped to Balkanize Europe's common international heritage into chaos and two world wars.

Rival Internationalists. The battle between right and right, as Lord Acton said, is more tragic than the battle between right and wrong. From an anti-militarist viewpoint, both Metternich and internationalist liberals were "right"; both sought a peaceful, cosmopolitan Europe. During 1789-1848, liberal middle-class internationalism and conservative aristocratic internationalism spent their energies in undermining—successfully undermining—each other's claims on Europe's loyalty. Wounding each other fatally in 1848, they created a vacuum of loyalty, which nationalism filled after 1870. Nationalism, not so innate nor so inevitable as sometimes believed, was perhaps merely the "lucky third" when the two rival internationalisms killed each other.

Many liberals combined internationalism with a liberal idealistic version of nationalism, such as the German Herder and the Italian Mazzini preached. Some liberals today consider the decision of liberals to ally with nationalists the fatal mistake of the nineteenth century. In a Europe of disputed national overlappings, a Europe of endless Alsace-Lorraines and Triestes, even the most liberal sort of nationalism could not assert its claims except by unliberal blood-and-iron methods.

"Conservative Socialism."   In 1831, a generation before Marx's *Das Kapital,* Metternich wrote: "The first instrument in the hands of the middle class is the modern representative system." He predicted that the next French Revolution would not be middle-class, as in the revolution of 1830, but proletarian. He warned that the French capitalists would suffer in twenty years the same revolution they were inflicting on the aristocracy in 1830. In the Paris of 1848 the warning came true. Would an exclusively middle-class liberalism turn out to be no more permanent as a base for an international Europe than had been the Holy Alliance of kings? Socialism was the base to which Metternich's thoughts occasionally turned as his aristocratic system approached its fall. In a letter of 1847 Metternich coined for himself the phrase "conservative socialist" (*"socialiste conservateur"*).

In unfamiliar eras the reader must expect unfamiliar use of familiar words. Thus the use by such monarchists of the antithesis "socialism" vs. "bourgeois *laisser-faire"* did not mean the economic systems today called "leftist." It meant an extension of the antithesis organic vs. atomistic (defined in Chapter 2): namely, *social* unity, monarchic *social* cement, and paternal *social* conscience vs. selfish *anti-social* individualism and commercialism. Aristocrats attributed the latter anti-social and atomistic qualities to the capitalist middle class and to the parliamentary, constitutionalist, *laisser-faire* liberals. In those days liberals were commonly associated with the middle class.

The professed aims of Metternich's "conservative

socialism" were peaceful, class-harmonizing, cosmopolitan, traditional. They must not be confused with the non-
peaceful, nontraditional aims of class-war Marxism and
with the violent, noncosmopolitan, racist aims of fascist
"national socialism." This monarchic socialism boiled
down to social paternalism, the monarch feeling a
"fatherly" duty to shield his flock from the rigors of
free economic forces. A concrete example was the Hapsburg relief program in Northern Italy. On such an issue,
the Emperor Francis and his minister agreed. In contrast
with the middle-class liberal credo of *laisser-faire,* this
monarchic program established humane public works and
social aid. The following is from Professor R. J. Rath's
scholarly monograph, "The Hapsburgs and the Great
Depression in Lombardy-Venetia, 1814-1818," *Journal of
Modern History,* September 1941 (italics added):

"By 1817, it was estimated that the funds which the
Austrian government had given for its public works program in Italy had enriched the poorer classes by Fr.
5,000,000. *The Austrian policy of taking care of the
destitute masses* in the Italian provinces by giving food
and money to those incapable of employment and providing a public works program for others, is in its general
outlines *surprisingly similar* to the public works and
emergency relief programs initiated in our own country
by the *Roosevelt* administration. . . . The actions of
Francis I, meager as they were in comparison with the
billion-dollar spending of our own times, did actually
save many persons from intense suffering. . . . The
financial condition of the Austrian government was so
precarious that actual bankruptcy was feared. In spite
of numerous difficulties, however, the Hapsburg monarch
did earnestly endeavor to *improve the lot* of his Italian
subjects, the hapless victims of a great depression."

Italy's liberal "revolutions" of the 1820's and 1830
were mainly limited to a small middle-class (and army
officer) minority, not representing the Italian masses.
The latter prospered more under Austrian rule than under
many of their various Italian princelings. Judging by his
private letters to intimates (Hübner, Rechberg, Prokesch-
Osten, and Wrede, some not found by scholars till 1928),
Metternich seemed sincere in his "conservative socialist"
view of liberalism and nationalism as a disguised middle-
class dictatorship over the masses. Demanding parlia-

ments and constitutions, most liberals of those days saw
only the political problem. He retorted: what really
counts is the "social problem." In 1849, while the victorious middle class was overthrowing kings, he added:
"I shall die . . . not as a politician but as a socialist."
These sentiments contradicted his admittedly more frequent reactionary behavior. Then were they intended
seriously? Or were they merely the epigram-loving pose
of a frivolous, easy-going *grand seigneur?* In either case,
they lived on triumphantly in England in his young
disciple, the future Prime Minister Disraeli (Chapter 6).

Influenced Disraeli. The two anti-middle-class
statesmen met in England after 1848 and became friends.
They even considered founding a pro-conservative periodical together. Disraeli called the old exile his "inspiration" and "dear master." It was partly owing to
Metternich that Disraeli renamed the "Tory" party "Conservative." The label stuck. Thus was Metternich's favorite word popularized in the English-speaking world, a
word Burke had never used and which (with several
exceptions) Tories had used infrequently compared to the
Continent. Metternich directly inspired a speech Disraeli
gave in Parliament denouncing nationalism as a dangerous
"newfangled principle." According to the standard biography of Disraeli (by Monypenny and Buckle), he also
borrowed from Metternich his argument that lovers of
liberty must support monarchy lest the alternative be not
a free democracy but the military dictatorship of plebeian
despots from below.

**Case Against Metternich: Reactionary Witch-
Hunter.** Disraeli's final characterization of Metternich:
"The only practical statesman who can generalize like a
philosopher. . . . Had he not been a Prince and Prime
Minister, he would have been a great Professor." Thus the
origins of the new view. But the reader, ever balancing
the pros and cons of conservatism, must assign equal or
more than equal weight to the old view. Its charges
against Metternich are extremely well documented: his
panicky exaggeration of Jacobin menaces everywhere; his
bullying repression of idealistic liberal revolutions in
Italy, of nationalist universities in Germany. Old view:
masking these crimes with the unctuous anti-liberal slan-
ders of Maistre and Burke, he sabotaged for half a century the onward march of progress.

— 12 (East of the Rhine) —

GERMANY

Goethe, Classicist. Johann Wolfgang Goethe (1749-1832) was Germany's greatest dramatist, poet, and personality. In his youthful "storm and stress" of the 1770's, Goethe went through a phase of revolt and of nationalism. In his old age, Goethe became Germany's greatest cultural influence for classical balance and for anti-nationalist cosmopolitanism. British thinkers likewise—Coleridge, Carlyle, Arnold—were influenced by him in the direction of conservatism; all three considered him one of the greatest sages of all time. After 1815, Goethe and Metternich had this in common: both took pride in being "good Europeans," not German nationalists. After a friendly personal conversation with Metternich, Goethe wrote: "It is encouraging . . . to be permitted to share the views of such a man who is directing the entire enormous complexity of questions, of which even a fragment would crush us others by its weight. Metternich is one of those who . . . inspires with the assurance that reason, reconciliation, and human understanding will lead us out of present chaos. . . . It is mastered by such able hands!"

Ever balanced, Goethe represented a mature synthesis between conservative framework and liberal goals. In 1830 he expressed that synthesis in terms still valid today: "The genuine liberal tries to achieve as much good as he can with the available means to which he is limited; but he would not use fire and sword to annihilate the often inevitable wrongs. Making progress at a judicious pace, he strives to remove society's deficiencies gradually without at the same time destroying an equal amount of good by violent measures. In this ever-imperfect world he contents himself with what is good until time and circumstances favor his attaining something better." His rhymed credo, "Nature and Art," 1802, expressed his conservative and classic stress on voluntary submission to law: "Only in self-restriction does the master reveal himself. And only law can give us liberty." His political drama, *The Natural Daughter,* 1803, reflected his hostility to the French Revolution, radicalism, and mass movements. Much quoted by classicists like America's Irving Babbitt was Goethe's definition: "The classical I call the healthy and the romantic the diseased." Yet his *Faust* drama (Part I published 1808; Part II, 1833) retained to the end the liberal-minded stress of his younger days on constant change, "constant striving" as salvation.

Goethe's most unique achievement consisted of his being, so to speak, self-invented. By sheer strength of character, he remolded his naturally revolutionary and romantic temperament into what the world accepted (not necessarily correctly) as a conservative and classicist temperament. Meanwhile he protected his very human sensitivity from the world by creating the inhuman "Goethe myth," the myth of the serene, remote Olympian. Subsequent German writers found it easier to imitate his myth than his genius. A whole lifetime of taming his own romantic rebelliousness he compressed into one intense epigram: "Everything that liberates the spirit without a corresponding growth in self-mastery is pernicious." That brief sentence remains an unequalled definition of classicism and conservatism.

Gentz (1764-1832). Two of the most important German conservative writers supporting the Metternich regime were Friedrich Gentz and Adam Müller. Gentz was Metternich's secretary, "brain trust," and friend and was nicknamed "Secretary of Europe" for his role in the Congress of Vienna. Gentz wrote articles attacking German nationalism as too aggressive and defending a league of nations and permanent peace as the basis for the settlement of 1815. (*See Document 7.*) How much Metternich's conservative ideas, especially his Burkean ones, are due to his secretary, Gentz, can never be calculated. It was Gentz who translated Burke's *Reflections on the Revolution* into German and established Burke as a lasting force in German intellectual life ever after.

Müller (1779-1829). Gentz's friend, Adam Müller, also ended up as a literary assistant to Metternich in Vienna. Müller carried to an anti-individualist extreme the conservative stress on organic vs. atomistic society. His book *Elements of Statecraft,* written 1808-1809, showed the influence of Gentz and Burke. An extreme anti-rationalism and the influence of Maistre may be found in Müller's essay *On the Necessity of a Theological Basis for All Political Science,* 1819. (*See Document 9.*) He was the leading political conservative produced by the anti-rational cultural movement of the early 1800's known as German romanticism, unless one wishes to classify the far greater philosopher, G. F. W. Hegel (1770-1831), as a conservative. But if Hegel's later defense of the Prussian monarchy was conservative, his stress on constant change in history was nothing of the sort and was later, when transferred to a materialist plane by Karl Marx, the philosophical basis of Marxist socialism. The philosophy of Hegel himself had best be called neither conservative nor anti-conservative but Hegelian. The most systematized Hegelian defense of Prussian conservatism came from his disciple, Julius Stahl (1802-1861).

Romantic Medievalism. Let us briefly summarize other ottantottist contemporaries of Müller. K. L. von Haller (1768-1854) published *Restoration of the Political Sciences,* 1816-1834. He performed for northern Germany the same function as Müller in Vienna—namely, the function of justifying a medieval union of church and state and "restoring" the pre-1789 legitimism. Joseph von Radowitz (1797-1853) was an extreme reactionary influencing the pro-medieval views of King Frederick William IV of Prussia. Bismarck called Radowitz "the clever keeper-of-the-wardrobe for the medieval fancies" of the king. Friedrich von Schlegel (1772-1829), originally a rebel, was a founder of the literary side of romanticism. Karl von Vogelsang (1816-1890) partly dominated conservatism in south Germany, also Vienna. Vogelsang's "social romanticism," like Müller's, pushed "organic" unity to authoritarian extremes. Vogelsang was an intellectual father of Austria's conservative and semi-authoritarian Christian Social party of the late nineteenth century; in 1934 that party culminated in an Austrian "corporative state," accused of "clerical fascism" by its opponents and overthrown by Hitler's annexation of Austria in 1938.

The five German conservatives—Müller, Haller, Radowitz, Schlegel, Vogelsang—had the following attitudes in common. They were more ottantottist than Burkean. They used Burke a great deal but were first of all German equivalents of Maistre and Bonald. At the same time they had more romantic vagueness, less French lucidity than Maistre and Bonald. These Germans all emerged from the romantic school. Accordingly, they loathed modern French rationalists and loved the Middle Ages. All five were Protestants to start with—and were all converted to Catholicism. Vague, emotional, and nostalgic, German romanticism seems the homesickness of Lutheranism for the lost Catholic Middle Ages.

Görres (1776-1848). As the clerical thought of German romanticism was largely a product of ex-Protestants, so its conservative thought was, to an insufficiently realized extent, the product of ex-Jacobins. Ex-Jacobins played a role in the ottantottism of the 1800's even more important than that of ex-communists in the American 1950's. Consider the career of Joseph von Görres, called "the most romantic among the Catholics." Like so many disillusioned supporters of the French Revolution (even Metternich's Gentz had at first supported it), Görres went over to the romantic school and extreme anti-rationalism. In his Jacobin period Görres had edited Germany's most revolutionary paper, *The Red Sheet,* 1790-1799. There he ridiculed religion and tradition, exalted the Rousseauistic "general will" of the masses. The invading French Revolutionists he lauded for overthrowing Germany's "barking packs of princes and hordes of clerics." With equal intemperance he became, after the usual disillusionment, Germany's most extreme defender of "princes and clerics." He now substituted the theocracy of Maistre for the democracy of his earlier hero, Rousseau. During 1814-1816, Görres edited the *Rhenish Mercury,* a leading organ of Catholic conservatism. Moderate Burke-style middle-roaders, whom as a Jacobin editor he had denounced as reactionary, he now denounced as too liberal; he, not they, had changed in the interval. He became professor of history at the University of Munich in Bavaria. There he influenced historical as well as political and religious thought through his "Görres Circle," 1837-1848.

Authoritarians in Germany and Austria after 1918 were partly influenced by the Görres Circle. For analysis of how German romanticism evolved from an anti-rational aesthetic movement into authoritarian politics, *cf.* longer studies like A. Kolnai's *War Against the West*, L. Snyder's *German Nationalism*, P. Viereck's *Metapolitics: From the Romantics to Hitler*. The romantic impulse—disorderly, wayward, subjective—ends by craving the pseudo-objectivity and pseudo-order of an extreme authoritarianism. Here, according to Irving Babbitt, is a conservatism not of classical balance but of hysteria and inner lack: the need of the jellyfish for the rock.

Savigny and Ranke. Germany's maturest conservative thought came not from her cloudy political philosophers nor from her ex-Jacobin romanticists but from her historians. They remain among the greatest historians in the world. F. K. von Savigny (1779-1861) and Leopold von Ranke (1795-1886) were outstanding as pupils of Burke in their reverence for history as organic growth. Savigny stressed that custom, operating over centuries, creates its own framework. On custom, Savigny founded an entire science of historical jurisprudence, denying the abstract, liberal "rights of man." Not deductive reasoning from rational premises but "history," argued Savigny "is the only true way to attain a knowledge of our own condition." His works include *History of Roman Law in the Middle Ages*, 1815-1831. Similarly Ranke saw every society in terms of its own unique evolution. He opposed the universal generalizations of eighteenth-century Enlightenment. Every people, he wrote, "is related directly to God" in its own concrete way. His books include *German History During the Reformation*, 1839-1847. Perhaps the most perfect example ever written of conservatism as the cult of history was his essay *Political Conversation*, 1836 (recently translated into English by Theodore von Laure).

Jakob Burckhardt (1818-1897). The Swiss Burckhardt and the German Nietzsche, friends and fellow-individualists, were both professors at the Swiss University of Basel. Later their concept of the "massman" was reapplied to the twentieth century by the Spanish philosopher José Ortega y Gasset (1883-1955) in his *Revolt of the Masses*, 1930. (*See Document 28.*) The reputation of the historian Burckhardt, during his own lifetime, rested on his *Civilization of the Renaissance in Italy*, 1885. The twentieth century brought him an additional reputation, based on his letters, as the conservative who foresaw totalitarianism. Universal suffrage and democratic equality would bring to power (he believed) the "terrible simplifiers" of a dictatorship more total than the old monarchies at their most despotic. For him as for most conservatives, the original villain was Rousseau: "Rousseau with his preaching of the goodness of human nature . . . resulted in the complete dissolution of the concept of [*legitimate*] authority" so that "naked force" would have to be the new and illegitimate authority of the future. (*See Document 16.*)

Friedrich Nietzsche (1844-1900). Nietzsche similarly predicted: "The democratising of Europe is at the same time an involuntary arrangement for the rearing of tyrants" (*Beyond Good and Evil*, 1886). The author of *Thus Spake Zarathustra*, 1883 ff., was too lyrically unpredictable to be called a conservative unless it be what Henry Adams called a "conservative anarchist." Nietzsche himself was pleased when a Danish critic called him an "aristocratic radical." However, he was second to none in furnishing valuable ammunition to conservatives by his insights into the mediocrity and conformity allegedly produced by liberal democracy and equality. His ammunition was not always used as intended. All too justified was his fear that some day he would be quoted, out of context, as a tool of German militarists and nationalists, whom he detested. It was not they he meant but a more spiritual self-discipline when he set up the "superman" ideal against the "herd" ideal and "master morality" against "slave morality." His prose and verse symbolize with unequaled beauty and depth the desperation of every artistic integrity trapped in a mechanized and soulless "herd." (*See Document 22.*)

Bismarck Era. Chapter 3 should be re-consulted as background for the German empire founded in 1871 by Otto von Bismarck (1815-1898). Nationalism and an economy of heavy industry replaced Metternich's cosmopolitan landed gentry as the new basis for conserving the *status quo*. Bismarck created an unphilosophical, opportunistic conservatism of power politics. By cloaking expediency with military glory, he harnessed together the German industrialists and the Prussian "Junkers" (authoritarian eastern landowners). This incongruous combination has characterized conservative political behavior in Germany ever since. Thus the middle class and the landed gentry avoided the domestic rivalry characterizing them in France and were able, instead, to unite behind a sabre-rattling foreign policy. Bismarck's heritage, the Prussianized German Empire of 1871-1918, achieved fabulous material success in both industrial and military power. But it produced no serious or lasting contributions to conservative or any other philosophy. As Nietzsche put it, referring to the title of the German national anthem: " 'Germany, Germany Over Everything,' I fear that has ended German philosophy." Intellect was sacrificed to power, and power stupefied its possessor.

Treitschke (1834-1896). After liberalism and Metternichian internationalism killed each other off in 1848, German conservatism adopted nationalism and narrowed down into power-worship and racial self-worship. Heinrich von Treitschke represented the Prussia-worshipping conservative wing of the "National Liberal" party, Bismarck's chief parliamentary support during 1866-1878. Treitschke's influential *German History in the Nineteenth Century,* 1879-1894, reviled the Metternich era. The Treitschke school of conservative nationalists found the more traditional conservatism of Prince Metternich too tolerant of Slavs and Jews, too peaceful and internationalist. Treitschke's anti-Semitism, anti-Catholicism, and cult of war foreshadowed the nazi climax of 1933-1945.

Under Weimar and Hitler. Under Germany's Weimar Republic, 1918-1933, much of the more intellectual opposition to democracy has been somewhat misleadingly called "the conservative revolution." Only a small minority thereof was truly conservative, later resisting Hitler and murdered by him. That ethical minority included Edgar Jung of the vaguely monarchist *Juniklub* ("June Club") and klaus von Stauffenberg of the élitist circle founded by the poet-prophet Stefan George (1868-1933). But a majority of the anti-democrats seemed less interested in conserving monarchy and tradition than in revolting on behalf of an untraditional right-wing dictatorship. Oswald Spengler (1880-1936), author of the monumental *Decline of the West* (1918-1922), glorified "Caesarism," authoritarian "Prussian socialism," and war ("Man is a beast of prey"). He despised democracy and the nazis alike, but admired the Italian fascist dictator, Benito Mussolini (1883-1945). Carl Schmitt (1888-   ), author of *Political Theology,* 1922 and *Concept of the Political,* 1933, became the ablest legal philosopher of totalitarianism. Schmitt drew heavily on the anti-liberal romanticism of Görres, Haller, and Adam Müller in vainly seeking a conservative justification for the romantic but unconservative Hitler.

The biggest internal attempt to overthrow the nazi reign of terror came from a group mainly conservative in credo and aristocratic in origin. Their plot of July, 1944 was too little and too late; a revolution while Germany was still winning the war would have seemed more impressively motivated. Yet the conservative aristocrats involved, including Germany's oldest families and highest army ranks, did die bravely under sadistic torture. Meanwhile, no uprising at all emerged from the liberal middle-class or from the Marxist-trained masses. Two generalizations tentatively suggest themselves: the record of conservative Germans for collaborating with the nazis was, with a few ethical exceptions, scandalous; the record of non-conservatives was no better. Presumably the post-Goethe and post-Metternich intoxication with nationalist power-politics in Germany had created moral callousness in all ranks, right and left alike.

Adenauer. Since then, the discrediting of German nationalism and of the Bismarck heritage in World War II has revived the older, more cosmopolitan conservatism of Goethe, Gentz, and Metternich. The post-war Chancellor Konrad Adenauer (in the words of Hans Kohn) "is the first great German statesman to look westward." Therein lies the hope of winning back German conservatism from the authoritarian anti-westernism of the Treitschkes and Schmitts.

— 13 (East of the Rhine) —

RUSSIA

Historical Uniqueness. Conservatism in the ordinary Western use of the term arose from reactions against the French Revolution. Tsarist conservatism, though also sharing these Western reactions, had basically different and older origins. Partly it went back to the autocratic Khans of the Tartars (Mongol rulers of Russia, 1240-1480). Partly it went back to the Greek Orthodox Church and to the medieval Byzantine empire of Constantinople, with its cult of divine autocracy. Serfdom, lack of middle class, and lack of constitutional traditions were other historical flukes promoting Russia's elephantiasis of autocracy. For all these reasons, Russian conservatism was unique. Its mystical, half-Byzantine, half-Asiatic cult of the monarch was too different to include, except briefly, in a book centering around Western conservatism.

Pobiedonostsev. Nevertheless, two anti-liberal traditionalists of Russia made such an impact on the West—the first by his politics, the second by his art—that their mention seems indispensable: Konstantin Pobiedonostsev (1827-1907) and Feodor Dostoyevsky (1821-1880). The former was the tutor of two tsars, Alexander III (ruled 1881-1894) and Nicholas II (ruled 1894-1917). During 1860-1865 he was professor of civil law at Moscow University. In 1880 he became chief procurator of the Holy Synod. During 1881-1905 he was backed by Alexander and Nicholas as the ideological dictator of Russia. Aged 79, he was ousted by the revolution of 1905.

Almost all Western conservatives, even a Maistre, were at least slightly influenced by liberalism despite themselves. But Pobiedonostsev retreated not one inch from his stubborn but intelligent and philosophical authoritarianism. To him the West and its strange notion called liberty were diabolical, being utterly unsuited to the special autocratic traditions of Russia. To him even the slightest hint of demands for a constitution was high treason. His book *Reflections of a Russian Statesman,* 1898, had at least a refreshing candor. It was free from the hypocrisies with which many Western conservatives unctuously protest how democratic they really are. It denounced free press, trial by jury, parliamentary government, secular education, scepticism towards the divine mission of tsars, and, above all, intellectuals.

In the last two paragraphs reprinted from his book (*see Document 23*), note how his sober philosophical tone suddenly changes to sheer lyric ecstasy when he describes autocratic power, which he calls simultaneously "sacred" and "terrifying." One can easily imagine a

Russian Bolshevik sharing the emotional power-cult of this Russian tsarist, product of six centuries of blending the practice of Tartar autocracy with the theory of Byzantine autocracy. Perhaps a Pobiedonostsev and a Russian Bolshevik are both, to some degree, the descendants of Ivan the Terrible (ruled 1533-1584), who first blended that Tartar practice with that Byzantine theory. In contrast, most Western conservatives and liberals alike, suspecting with Lord Acton that "all power tends to corrupt," would have shuddered at Pobiedonostsev's passage of autocratic ecstasy.

Dostoyevsky. Dostoyevsky's disillusionment with his youthful radicalism resembled Coleridge's in its psychological as well as literary consequences. Both turned to an organic, religious, and monarchic society, to which they paid more homage via literature than via politics. Dostoyevsky attacked socialism, liberalism, materialism, and atheism. He preached Greek Orthodox tsarism, Slavic traditionalism, and the redemption of mankind by "Holy Russia." His novel *The Possessed,* 1871, pictured the idealistic ends of socialists as corrupted by their terroristic means. He boasted somewhat fawningly to Alexander III about his book's effectiveness against radicals. His novel *The Brothers Karamazov,* 1879, contrasted a dry Western rationalism with a more deeply moving Russian mysticism. His two anti-liberal periodicals, *The Citizen,* 1873 ff. and *Diary of a Writer,* were guided by close personal consultations every week with none other than Pobiedonostsev, "whose wisdom," wrote Dostoyevsky, "I deeply respect."

Yet he was vastly more than a propagandist for the *status quo*. In contrast with the despotic *status quo,* he retained from his young socialist days his characteristic compassion for what he called "the insulted and injured"; only now he expressed this in the more spiritual creed of Christian love. Some critics deem it blasphemous to speak of so great a novelist in political terms at all. What influences modern readers so compellingly is not his political but his cultural conservatism, exalting our vision beyond external material progress. (*See Document 17.*)

V THE UNITED STATES

— 14 —

OUR FEDERALIST FOUNDERS: THE CONSERVATION OF 1776

Burkean Spirit of 1776. The American Revolution reflected England's heritage of 1688, the heritage of mature self-government. Never were our Burkean founding fathers more British than when they were revolting against George III. Burke favored their Revolution as defending the traditional rights of freeborn Englishmen against new-fangled royal usurpations. In that sense, we may re-christen it not the Revolution but the Conservation of 1776. The firecrackers of July Fourth celebrate the triumph not of revolution but of restoration.

In *Rights of the British Colonies*, 1764, the American spokesman James Otis (1725-1783) typically argued that our demand for no taxation without representation was an old British tradition. America, he said, was conserving "the British Constitution, the most free one on earth"; England was the radical subverting it. "We claim nothing," added George Mason of Virginia, "but the liberty and privileges of Englishmen." Almost all other revolutions, colonial or otherwise, have been radical in the sense of demanding new or increased liberties and a new order. In contrast, the American demand of July 6, 1776 (*Declaration of Causes of Taking Up Arms*) was for conserving old liberties and the old order: "in defense of the freedom that is our birthright and which we ever enjoyed till the late violation of it." Such words promulgated no democracy, no abstract "Rights of Man"; rather, they promulgated what Burke called "prescriptive right . . . considering our liberties in the light of an inherit-ance." Despite important exceptions, it was not until the election of the more truly "revolutionary" Jackson, 1828, that the new democratic doctrines of Paine gained solid roots in America, dividing the nation between conserva-tive and progressive traditions ever since. Paine was the man John Adams came to loathe most: for eternally sloganizing about *a priori* utopias.

In contrast with the liberal 1930's, several major historians of the 1950's like Daniel Boorstin and Clinton Rossiter are rediscovering our conservative origins. In *The Genius of American History,* 1953, Boorstin observes: "The ablest defender, the greatest political theorist of the American Revolution was also the great theorist of British conservatism, Edmund Burke. . . . Ours was one of the few conservative colonial rebellions of modern times." Analyzing the theory of our founders in his prize-winning *Seedtime of the Republic,* 1953, Rossiter concludes: "Perhaps the most remarkable characteristic of this political theory was its deep-seated conservatism."

Seven Classics of Conservatism. The spirit of America was partly molded by two masterpieces of Burkean conservatism, both published 1787-1788: *The Federalist* by Alexander Hamilton (1757-1804), James Madison (1751-1836), and John Jay (1745-1829), and *Defense of the Constitutions* by John Adams (1735-1826). (*See Documents 2, 3, 4.*) The achievements attributed by historians to the *Federalist* papers exceed those of any other series of newspaper articles in history. They won American opinion to accept the Constitution. They forged a close-knit unity during a separatist crisis. In the context of the Shays Rebellion of 1786 against the judiciary, they saved government by law from government by mob. They established minority rights against majority dictatorship. They based American liberty on the Burkean principle of concrete roots, prescriptive right, and judicial precedent instead of on vague, grand rhetoric about democratic utopias and the masses. Similar in thought and richer in historical background was the *Defense* by Adams, one of the most sustained analyses of self-government ever written. Two lesser classics by Adams were *Thoughts on Government,* 1776 and *Discourses on Davila,* 1791, refuting direct democracy.

Next came *Letters of Publicola,* 1791, by his son J. Q. Adams (1767-1846). (*See Document 5.*) These *Letters* chided Jefferson for sponsoring Paine's rebuttal to Burke; they defended the old British Constitution as a model for America, as against Paine's defense of the Revolutionary French Constitution. A sixth classic was Washington's Farewell Address of 1796. It justified his conservative policies against his radical critics. It appealed for an organic unity not atomized by party rivalry.

Seventh came the posthumous *Madison Papers* of 1840. They were conservative in their philosophy of human nature and of indirect democracy even though Madison, after his famous break with Hamilton, became a Jeffersonian liberal in terms of actual political parties.

These seven masterworks of sober liberty and lawful self-government constitute one of the most substantial bodies of conservative thought produced by any country in the world. Likewise one of the oldest. The first three works (1787-1788 and 1776) antedate the works of almost all European conservatives: Maistre's, Metternich's, and even Burke's *Reflections* of 1790. It is European conservatism that is young and new, judging by the actual *dates* of the documents in Part II, and American conservatism which is old and rooted! Nevertheless, many of the ablest authorities prefer instead to speak of something called "America's revolutionary tradition," which America allegedly "betrays" by today being mankind's strongest remaining bulwark against Soviet world revolution. Undoubtedly some early American radical writer— Paine, Freneau, Patrick Henry, Sam Adams, R. H. Lee— can be matched against each of the foregoing early conservative writers. Present-day Americans must then decide for themselves which side in the matched pairs is of greater historic stature and more representative.

Liberty via Aristocracy. Hamilton, Adams, and their Federalist party sought to establish in the new world what they called a "natural aristocracy," based on property, education, family status, and sense of ethical responsibility. Being founders of a nation without titles or feudal past, they could hardly establish any other aristocracy than an untitled "natural" one. In a country where recently a newly founded college, a week old, could hold a meeting to vote itself "some ancient traditions," it seems not ironic but only normal that the two main founders of "rule by the well-born" were an illegitimate pauper educated by charity (Hamilton) and a lad whose family social status was at first so low (Adams) that Harvard denied him the high academic classification he had rightfully earned.

Yet the motive of Hamilton and Adams, in establishing a new aristocracy, was not merely an overcompensation for humiliation. Nor was it merely material gain. Their motive was liberty itself. Just as Burke made British liberty depend on inequality and on a parliament of noblemen, so Adams argued in 1790: "The nobles have been essential parties in the preservation of liberty . . . against kings and people." It does our Federalist founders an injustice and misses the spirit of their age if their love of élitist inequality is treated separately from their love of liberty. As for "the people," they were not, as today, deemed guardians of freedom but (in Hamilton's phrase) "a great beast."

Adams spoke for many Federalists in 1789 (the very moment of the anti-monarchic Revolution in France) when he called America "a monarchical republic, a limited monarchy" owing to the special role of the president. He called the presidency, though elective, as exalted as old-world royalty. Consequently, the Federalists sought to give the presidency the pomp and ceremony surrounding kings. For such views, Adams, our second president, and his son, our sixth president, were denounced by the Democratic party as "monarchists" and as America's hereditary "House of Stuart." Yet their ideal was never monarchy, never any reminder of the hated George III, but "a free republic." The Adamses, Hamilton, and Madison used "democracy" to mean direct democracy, "republic" to mean indirect democracy (defined in Chapter 2). They stressed that "a republic" and "liberty" depended on what Hamilton called "sacred reverence toward the Constitution." Such reverence seems an emotional transfer of that felt for kings, making the American Constitution a sublimated monarchy. Adams warned his radical second cousin, Sam Adams: "The multitude as well as the nobles must have a check." The check was to be this mystically revered Constitution. Pure democracy had no check on its majority passions. Therefore, said Adams, "there never was a democracy yet that did not commit suicide."

Our Conservative Constitution. Our Constitution was drawn up by the Philadelphia Convention of 1787. The objectives of many liberal democrats were: easy amendments, facilities for mass pressure and rapid change, unchecked popular sovereignty, universal manhood suffrage, only one parliamentary body, and the basing of liberty on a long list of universal *a priori* abstractions, such as Burke later criticized in the French "Rights of Man." But in our Constitution of 1787 the Federalists foiled each objective. They made amendments slow and difficult, greatly reduced the number of voters by property restrictions, created a Congress of two parliamentary bodies, and based liberty primarily, though not entirely, on the concrete, inherited precedents of British tradition. Except for the House of Representatives (a sop to democrats), the main cogs of government—President, Senate, Justices—were not to be chosen directly by the people but respectively by the electoral college, state legislatures, and appointment. Not until 1913 did an amendment eliminate this intentionally undemocratic election of senators. Even today the principle of judicial review keeps the Constitution aristocratic, not democratic. The judicial branch (Supreme Court) is non-elective, non-removable, an élite not responsible to democratic majorities. Yet it can veto as unconstitutional the measures passed by a democratic majority of the two elective, removable branches of Congress. In other words the tyranny-hating creators of our Constitution accepted Adams' key hypothesis that "the people [*are*] as tyrannic as any king."

Why did the founders adopt a Constitution so conservative and so concrete? They were reacting against current mob excesses and against the democratic-utopian rhetoric of the earlier Declaration of Independence (drawn up by Jefferson) with its grand abstractions about "life, liberty, and the pursuit of happiness." Justifying the Constitution and Senate as watchdogs against democracy, John Adams wrote: "The rich . . . have as clear and as sacred a right to their large property as others have to theirs which is smaller. . . . The rich, therefore, ought to have an effective barrier in the Constitution against being robbed . . . and this can never be without an independent Senate." No wonder anti-Federalists like R. H. Lee of Virginia damned "this new Constitution" as "dangerously oligarchic."

Yet, our Constitution was the Burkean, not the reactionary brand of conservatism. Thus, it defeated not only the liberal objectives but also the more extreme conservative ones, including a hereditary, titled aristocracy and Hamilton's notion of a president-for-life with absolute veto power, in effect a king. The more moderate conservatism of 1787 was best represented by neither Jeffersonian liberals nor Hamiltonian right-wingers but by Madison and Adams. Their middle-road solution placed sane checks and balances not only on Jeffersonian democracy but also on Hamiltonian aristocracy. For, in the immortal words of Adams, "Absolute power intoxicates alike despots, monarchs, aristocrats, and democrats. . . ." Our Constitution's moderate conservatism seems best expressed by Madison's tenth *Federalist* paper (*Document 4*). It argued for "the advantage a republic has over a democracy." By democracy, he meant unchecked majority rule; by a republic, representative government protecting minority rights. Thereby Madison prevented what he called the "excess of democracy" of "men without property and principle." "Property," argued our founders, gives roots and a sense of responsibility to our "natural aristocrats"; it must be protected from demagogue-incited majorities. But defense of property did not mean hucksterism, nor plutocracy, nor the spirit of W. G. Sumner (see page 99). Adams denounced "the spirit of commerce and avarice" as strongly as he defended lawful rights of property.

The Case Against Our Founding Fathers. The stability which the Constitution of 1787 achieved for years to come (one of the longest-lasting constitutions in history) may be contrasted with the instability that followed the more democratic, anti-conservative French Constitution of only two years later. Thus reason proponents of the founding fathers. Opponents reason: their lip-service to stability and liberty merely concealed (as the historian Charles Beard sometimes implied) their greedy economic self-interest. Their Constitution, in radical and Marxist eyes, was a conspiracy to frustrate, with checks and delays and indirect elections, the holy will and welfare of the masses, whose more enlightened expression was not the reactionary American Revolution but the progressive French Revolution, falsely slandered as terroristic by smug Federalist millionaires like George Washington.

Religion. Our conservative founders were forever cautioning utopians against what Hamilton called "the depravity of human nature." Men are "not angels," wrote Madison. He based his restrictions of majority rule upon "the depravities of the human character." "Whoever would found a state," warned Adams, "must presume that all men are bad by nature." Human goodness, retorted the semi-Rousseauistic Jefferson, "is innate." Despite some notable exceptions, conservatives tended toward formal and institutionalized forms of Protestantism—"national morality," said Washington, depends on religion—while liberals like Jefferson and the more extreme Paine tended toward Deism. Deism was the optimistic, vaguely benevolent belief of many eighteenth-century intellectuals in a non-Christian clockmaker-God and in a universe as geometric, rational, and benign as an eighteenth-century garden. (Cf. F. Wilson's able *Case for Conservatism*.)

Adams Plus Jefferson. "The first time that you and I differed in opinion," wrote Adams to his friend and rival Jefferson, ". . . was the French Revolution." It divided Americans even more passionately than the later Russian Revolution. Nevertheless, both statesmen had more principles linking them than holding them apart. Jefferson wrote Adams that he, too, believed in "natural aristocracy among men" and in whatever society could "provide the most effectively for a pure selection of these *aristoi* into the office of government." In turn, Adams's ultimate goal was neither property nor aristocracy (mere means to his goal) but liberty, conserved from "tyranny, delirious tyranny, wherever it was placed," monarchic, democratic, or aristocratic. And in this noble goal America's wisest conservative and America's wisest liberal were fraternally united when both departed from life on the same symbolic day of 1826: the Fourth of July.

Hamilton vs. Jefferson. In 1787 young Hamilton told the framers of our Constitution: "All communities divide themselves into the few and the many. The first are the rich and well-born, the other the mass of the people. . . . The people are turbulent and changing. . . . Give, therefore, to the first class a distinct, permanent share in the government. They will check the unsteadiness of the second." Jefferson, in turn, summed up the American liberal tradition: "I am not among those who fear the people." Yet history is more complex; the lines between conservative and liberal cannot be drawn so simply as that. Jefferson and Adams joined in rejecting Hamilton's emphasis on economics and on a centralized national economy crushing local traditions. Such statism seems closer to the "planners" of the modern left than to normal conservatism. In *The Conservative Mind*, 1953, Russell Kirk wisely calls Hamilton "not really a conservator of old ways but a planner of a new order." Jefferson resembled the agrarian traditionalism of European conservatives when he opposed Hamilton's rationalistic, *a priori* blueprints for an industrialized, urbanized America, regimented by lords of commerce. Jefferson was the truer conservative of the two when he wrote in *Notes on Virginia:* "The mobs of great cities add just so much support of pure government as sores do to the strength of the human body."

Federalist Party.   Hamilton and Adams founded the Federalist party; Jefferson, the Democratic party (named "Republican" in those days). Although the Democrats preached eighteenth-century liberalism, in practice both parties of our founders (prior to the Jacksonian revolution of 1828) belonged to a small and highly privileged élite. The Federalists belonged to a New England élite of merchant-princes; the Democrats to a southern élite of plantation-owners and propertied, precedent-rooted lawyers. (In 1835 Tocqueville called these lawyers "America's natural aristocrats.") Both parties were united in leading and educating rather than echoing the mass will. Both opposed universal suffrage. Even the liberal Jefferson, himself a landed country gentleman, favored restricting the vote to taxpayers and militia. Swarming with varlets in livery, bowing and scraping lackeys, and overawed cap-in-hand petitioners, the palaces of many of our founding fathers—Jefferson's may still be visited at Williamsburg—hardly looked like log cabins. (In a somewhat misleading contrast with the lavish style of Washington and Jefferson, the frugal simplicity of our more New-England-style founders was actually *still* more aristocratic but in a subtler sense: Anglo-Saxon understatement and a rich man's conspicuous abstention from "conspicuous waste.") These American *grands seigneurs* were neither coon-capped Davy Crocketts nor folksy tribunes of the plebs. Yet many Europeans and some Americans still view their Constitutional Convention of 1787 as some powwow of Rousseauistic "noble savages."

The fact that America was founded on a restricted suffrage, on a Constitution checking majority rule, and on a closed hierarchical "government by gentlemen"— that fact may suggest, as did the undemocratic parliament of Burkean England, that liberty and free speech may go at least as well with aristocracy as with democracy. The fact that both parties of our founders in practice, and one of them also in explicit theory, preferred inequality to democracy did not make their early America less free than today's. On the contrary (allege conservatives), that fact allowed their early America more individual freedom than does the tyrannic mass-conformity of today.

How then did two such equally élitist parties differ? In the ninth *Federalist* paper (*Document 3*), Hamilton argued that only a strong central government could maintain unity and protect property. Thus, the Federalists favored strong, the Democrats weak, government. But even that party difference seems more opportunistic than real, for it was reversed during Jefferson's administration (1801-1809). Ever since, the outs in America have usually backed state rights; the ins, centralization. In foreign policy, though again inconsistently, the Federalists favored monarchic England over Revolutionary France; the Democrats, the opposite. Deeper than these shifting improvisations of politics was the difference in temperament. The Jeffersonian temperament was optimistic, trusted human nature. "Jefferson," scoffed the Federalist Gouverneur Morris (1752-1816), "believes in the perfectibility of man, the wisdom of mobs, and the moderation of Jacobins." The Federalist temperament was forever predicting doom. Federalist Fisher Ames (1758-1808) incorrectly predicted in 1807 that "our disease, democracy," would speedily kill America.

George Washington (1732-1799) openly favored the Federalist party. It dominated young America's formative years: the Administrations of Washington and then of Adams, together covering 1789-1801. Thereafter it dwindled away into mere New England separatists. It was killed by many factors: the inner feud between President Adams and Hamilton; the distrust of the anti-aristocrats, Anglophobes, and Francophiles; its own hysterical Alien and Seditions Acts of 1798. (In a friendly letter to Jefferson, Adams later disowned the excesses of these thought-control Acts and blamed them on the intolerant Hamilton.) The party died, its principles lived on—in other parties under other names. Its conservative principle of Constitutional and judicial checks on mob rule has reappeared today, under a more democratic terminology to suit a more democratic age.

CALHOUN

Calhoun (1782-1850). John Calhoun, champion of Southern aristocracy, is being increasingly rediscovered today as America's most original political theorist. He combined profound political philosophy with practical politics. That combination was not to recur in American history. Subsequent conservative men of action did not bother with a theoretical justification, while subsequent conservative theorizers have usually been intellectuals far removed from political office. Hence the uniqueness and importance of Calhoun in American conservatism: the last knowing doer and doing knower. His two chief essays, published after his death in 1850, were *A Disquisition on Government* and its longer sequel, *A Discourse on the Constitution and Government of the United States*. The former defended minority rights against majority dictatorship by his doctrine of "concurrent majority." The latter defended state rights against central government. The stain on his otherwise ethical leadership was his defense of slavery. That defense had not been shared by the abolitionist Burke and by earlier conservatives like the Federalists. It reflected the intense sectional hates preceding the Civil War and the increasingly defensive position of the South.

Calhoun became chief representative of the Southern conservative wing of the Democratic party. He was variously Senator from South Carolina, Secretary of War, twice Vice President, twice almost President. He was elected Vice President first in 1824, again in 1828. In 1824 he had to serve under his enemy President J. Q. Adams; in 1828 under his enemy President Andrew Jackson (1767-1845). It was a three-cornered fight, each detesting the other two: the Southern conservative Calhoun, the Southern liberal Jackson, the anti-slavery Yankee conservative Adams.

Jacksonian Revolution. Finally, Jackson (his dar-

ing new slogan: "the supremacy of the people's will")
defeated Calhoun and J. Q. Adams alike. Thereupon,
America left the élitist conservative era of its founders
and entered the new era of mass democracy. An era of
mass conformity, mass mediocrity, and mob tyranny,
warned Calhoun and J. Q. Adams alike. An era of the
greatest liberty and greatest material progress in history,
retorted the triumphant egalitarians.

The Jacksonian revolution was backed above all by
the new unconservative West, with its faith in an idealized
a priori abstraction called "the common man." As if
Original Sin could cease at the Alleghenies. Or as if a
semi-Rousseauistic West could dissolve the Burkean contract with the past without suffering from two retributions
ever after: demagogy and a cultureless materialism. Such
were the allegations— perhaps entirely incorrect ones—of
conservatism.

Part Ottantottist, Part Burkean. By defending traditional local rights, Calhoun was closer to his hero Burke
than were those earlier Burkeans, the centralizing Federalists. For Burke had taught the primacy of loyalty to
one's own local "little platoon." On the other hand, Calhoun went to greater extremes than Burke or the Federalists in opposing change and wanting, in his own term,
to "restore" a lost past. As restorationist, he was not
Burkean but America's closest equivalent of the ottantottist Maistre. Maistre and Burke would both have approved
Calhoun's insistence that freedom springs not from
rational, *a priori* blueprints but from the blind, slow,
organic growth of history. Thus, Calhoun, during the
Mexican war of 1846-1848, denounced America's messianic ambition "to spread civil and religious liberty over
all the globe" and argued instead: ". . . There is scarcely
an instance of a free constitutional government which
has been the work exclusively of foresight and wisdom.
They have all been the result of a fortunate combination
of circumstances."

Defining "Concurrent Majority." Calhoun's subtle
doctrine of concurrent majority, more often cited by
historians than clearly defined, justified Southern state
rights against the anti-Southern national majority. Here is
how he himself defined the doctrine. "Concurrent or
constitutional majority," opposed to democratic dictatorship, "regarded interests as well as numbers, considering

the community made up of different and conflicting interests." Therefore, never trample on one of these basic interests, even when it happens to be in a numerical minority. For "the sense of the entire community" includes the mutual respect these basic interests, minority or majority, must have for each other. "It is this mutual negative among its various conflicting interests which invests each with the power of protecting itself." His opponents, the Jacksonian Democrats, argued: if a democratic numerical majority can be vetoed by such a minority interest, the result will be an impossible deadlock and paralysis. No, counter-argued Calhoun, there will then be progress through "compromise." For him, "compromise" and "concurrent majority" were the two-fold "conservative principle of constitutional governments."

Southern vs. Northern Conservatism. Democratic government by a numerical rather than concurrent majority would mean not liberty but a tyranny of North over South: "a single section [*the North*], governing by the will of the numerical majority, has now, in fact, the control of the government . . . as absolute as that of the autocrat of Russia and as despotic. . . . The South possesses no means by which it can resist." (Speech of March 4, 1850.) In these words Calhoun established what would later become the Southern cause in the Civil War. That lost cause, justified philosophically by "concurrent majority" and "state rights," was the second great conservative movement in our history. The first had been the Federalists. Both were rooted in a regional aristocracy: the first, New England and centralizing; the second, Southern and decentralizing. Both preferred liberty to equality, Burke to Paine. Then came the Civil War between them, followed by a new situation submerging both: modern industrialism.

AMERICA SINCE THE CIVIL WAR

Business or anti-business: which side in modern industrialism is the legitimate heir of America's conservative origins? The best authorities still disagree; let us summarize the positions of both sides.

Sumner, 1840-1910. After the Civil War of 1861-1865, agrarian aristocrats were replaced by an industrial élite. Its chief philosophical proponent was Professor W. G. Sumner of Yale: "The millionaires are a product of natural selection, acting on the whole body of men, to pick out those who can meet the requirement of certain work to be done. . . . They get high wages and live in luxury, but the bargain is a good one for society" (1902). Author of the pro-industrialist *History of American Currency,* 1874 and of the anti-utopian *Folkways,* 1907, he acclaimed unrestricted laisser-faire competition not as a robber-baron era but as a superhuman law of nature: "The social order is fixed by laws of nature precisely analogous to those of the physical order. . . . The law of the survival of the fittest is not man-made and can not be abrogated by man." (*See Document 25.*)

Social Darwinism Plus Manchester Liberalism. Already before 1850, Calhoun had vainly warned the North: its tradesmen might follow their suppression of the aristocratic agrarian South by suppressing the working class in the North itself. After the Civil War, the victorious Northern tradesmen did indeed clash with Northern workers and Western farmers. So doing, the tradesmen worked out a new philosophy, combining the *laisser-faire* economics of the "Manchester liberals" with the "Social Darwinism" of the British philosopher Herbert Spencer (1820-1903). The Manchester liberals were a school popularizing, in the British Liberal party, the *laisser-faire* capitalism of Adam Smith (1723-1790). Spencer's Social Darwinism may be defined as applying to human society, in an analogy never approved by Darwin himself, the ruthless, competitive "survival of the fittest" that Darwin had found in animal biology.

Social Darwinism and Manchester *laisser-faire* both envisage an atomistic society, not an organic one. They envisage a rootless individualism, not a harmonizing traditionalism. Therefore, they are not only against socialism on the left but against organic conservatism and traditional aristocracy on the right. Opponents say: the combination of Social Darwinism and *laisser-faire* leads to cash-nexus plutocracy. Proponents say: it leads to democracy, history's highest living standards of all, and an equality of opportunity for rising into a new "natural aristocracy" of tradesmen, as first advocated by Hamilton.

Business Spokesmen. Whether you choose to call that school Social Darwinism, Manchester liberalism, or a special American variation of conservatism, its most influential ideologist in America was W. G. Sumner, as summarized earlier. Its practical political expression has been the Old Guard wing of the Republican party, as represented by William McKinley (President 1897-1901) and later by Senator Robert A. Taft (1889-1953). Its best known principles are "rugged individualism" and "free enterprise." Its most widely circulated popularization was Elbert Hubbard's *Message to Garcia,* 1899. Hubbard denounced "maudlin sympathy" for workers in slums. He urged a presumably unmaudlin sympathy for "the employer who grows old before his time in a vain attempt to get frowsy ne'er-do-wells to do intelligent work." On a level of incomparably higher intellect and idealism stands F. A. Hayek, author of *The Road to Serfdom,* 1944, and one of today's leading philosophers of capitalist *laisser-faire.*

Trade Unions. Reacting against such an atomistic view of society, still more recent conservatives prefer to restore, via the trade union, the organic community symbolized by the medieval guild. The old spirit of warm, human cooperation is thereby to replace the cold, inhuman "cash-nexus" (*cf.* Carlyle in Chapter 5). "Trade unionism," writes the American scholar Frank Tannenbaum in *A Philosophy of Labor,* 1952, "is the conservative movement of our time. It is the counter-revolution. . . . It denies the [*atomistic*] heritage that stems from the French Revolution and from English [*laisser-faire*] liberalism." (*See Document 30.*) Such thinkers are an

American equivalent of the organic views of Coleridge and Disraeli and of the semi-socialist, semi-feudal medievalism of Ruskin. They are a minority in American conservatism. They will continue to be a minority, mainly intellectuals, so long as trade unionists remain blissfully indifferent to being "the conservative counter-revolution." In contrast, the vast majority of Americans who believe themselves (not necessarily with accuracy) to be conservatives and natural aristocrats are still in the Sumner Republican camp.

Republicans vs. Democrats. The post-Civil War era is still too recent and debatable for authorities to decide which of two rival groups are the "true" conservatives and aristocrats: (1) the business community and the Republican party; (2) those who distrust the business community as atomistic and rootless and who prefer (in the style of Disraeli's "Tory democracy") the Democratic party's alliance of southern agrarian aristocrats and social-minded northern trade unions. Under labels less paradoxical and with special American roots, the old Metternich-Disraeli formula of *"socialiste conservateur"* has partly re-appeared in the New Deal. The New Deal allied the trade unions with the social and intellectual aristocracy represented by "the squire of Hyde Park." The Roosevelts were a family of old Duchess County landowners resembling the Adamses as producers of presidents; already the "trust-buster" Theodore Roosevelt, Republican President 1901-1909, had called Big Business "glorified pawnbrokers" whose newfangled plebeian "materialism" betrayed America's nobler, older traditions. Franklin D. Roosevelt, Democratic President 1933-1945, created the New Deal alliance of workers, intellectuals, and anti-huckster "high society," cutting short the post-Civil War attempt at a Sumner-style natural aristocracy of businessmen.

The modern Republican businessman may be regarded as the descendant, no longer revolutionary but now respectable, of the French Revolution. The French Revolution of 1789 had brought to power the anti-aristocratic, commercial middle class. The Revolution had proclaimed (among other things) an atomistic society of *laisser-faire* liberalism and economic free enterprise against the state-controls of an organic, monarchic society. According to this debatable hypothesis, the *laisser-faire* capitalists represent the French Revolution, while the New Deal has made conservatism possible again, even though doing so unintentionally. An equally well-documented hypothesis says just the opposite: the radical segments of the New Deal, its utopian abstractions and faith in the masses, were descended from the revolutionary Jacobins, while the solid, cautious, reliable businessmen represent the Burkean counter-revolution. The reader will have to weigh both hypotheses and decide for himself.

What of the future? Will not an increasingly mellowed business world evolve a conservatism as profound as that of the vanished landed aristocrats (and their Burkean or Coleridgean spokesmen) and economically more productive? Only time can answer this completely open question. Meanwhile, extremely intelligent editorials on conservatism, not blind toward social justice, are appearing in the *Wall Street Journal* (*see Document 31*), *Fortune* magazine, and the Republican *New York Herald-Tribune;* the latter's chief editorial writer since 1952 has been the distinguished "New Conservative" August Heckscher. Such voices and that of the C.E.D. (Committee for Economic Development) are the measure of how far some American businessmen have matured (since robber-baron days) toward a responsible statesmanship and toward a *noblesse oblige* that is not plutocratic but truly aristocratic.

Cultural Conservatives: Melville, Hawthorne. But, although a narrowly political conservatism in America may today require such a business élite, conservatism need not be political at all. Instead, its characteristic American form may be a lonely soul-searching by American artists to transcend what Melville called "the impieties of progress." Many of America's greatest literary figures have been cultural conservatives in their anti-optimism, their qualms about external reforms—for example, James Fenimore Cooper (1789-1851), Nathaniel Hawthorne (1804-1864), Edgar Allan Poe (1809-1849), Herman Melville (1819-1891), Henry James (1843-1916), William Faulkner (1897-   ). Hyatt Waggoner's *Hawthorne,* 1955, represents the latest research of those scholars who see the real American cultural tradition as a conservative "tragic sense," affirming Original Sin and rejecting liberal illusions about progress and human nature. These liberal illusions, concludes Waggoner, "were useless for any artist who would not wilfully blind himself to the existence of tragedy. . . . The 'evolutionary optimism' of . . . nineteenth-century liberalism was affronted by anyone who concerned himself with the 'deeper psychology.' " On the campuses, this non-political conservatism is already leading a counter-movement against "progressive education" and its optimistic view of human nature and is returning to the literary and religious classics of a more tradition-rooted wisdom. The ideal inspiring America's cultural conservatives has been best expressed by a little-known quatrain of Melville:

> "Not magnitude, not lavishness,
> But Form—the site;
> Not innovating wilfulness,
> But reverence for the Archetype."

Henry Adams, 1838-1918. Four generations of the Adams family almost embodied a history of American conservatism in itself: President John Adams, his son President J. Q. Adams, his grandson Ambassador Charles Francis Adams, his great-grandson Henry Adams. A Rousseauistic Populist liberal from out West might call these Boston Brahmins "reactionary snobs." A Calhounian Southerner might call them "radicals" for being so militant against slavery. Yet they did represent conservatism in their distrust of democratic optimism and human nature. The fourth Adams expressed this distrust in his novel *Democracy*, 1880, and in his autobiography, *The Education of Henry Adams*, 1906. The novel described the inevitable corruption of a too-optimistic democratic idealism, as symbolized by a homespun Midwest Senator; the prediction is made that American democracy, having lost the aristocracy of its founding fathers, "will be more corrupt than Rome under Caligula." The *Education*, today a literary classic, revealed much the same moral sensibility and cultural conservatism as the novels of Hawthorne and Melville. Adams insisted almost petulantly upon a typically conservative antithesis: the "true" America, founded by his own aristocratic ancestors, versus the post-Civil War plutocracy under Grant (President 1869-1877). In 1911 Adams wrote his brother that the Grant industrial plutocracy "wrecked the last chance of lifting society back to a reasonably high plain."

Irving Babbitt and Paul Elmer More. Historians increasingly look not to modern politicians and parties but to Irving Babbitt (1865-1933) and to Paul Elmer More (1864-1930) as the legitimate heirs of our classic conservatives of the Federalist Papers. Babbitt was Professor of French Literature at Harvard. He founded the modern "humanist" movement with More. More was author of the *Shelburne Essays,* 1904 *ff.*, and a leading literary critic. Their use of the ambiguous word "humanism" meant a cultural and ethical conserving of values, based on literary classicism. Thereby, their movement resembled the ideals elsewhere noted under Goethe, Coleridge, and Arnold. Babbitt's *Rousseau and Romanticism,* 1919, the Bible of American classicists, attacked romanticism for its emotional self-indulgence and for the cultural as well as political radicalism inherent in its lack of inner ethical rigor. Opponents retorted: the Babbitt-More attack misrepresented the romantics and Rousseau. In any case, it sometimes seemed to attack the romantics with a romantic intemperance. Yet its main points held.

The warnings of the Federalists and then of Calhoun against democratic tyranny received their third great American expression in Irving Babbitt's book, *Democracy and Leadership,* 1924. It glorified traditional, nonelective, partly aristocratic institutions like the Supreme Court and distinguished between direct and constitutional democracy. Babbitt traced direct democracy back to Rousseau and Jefferson, based on their illusions about human nature. He traced constitutional democracy back to Burke and George Washington, restricting the mass will. (*See Document 27.*)

Babbitt fought on two fronts. On the right of him, he resisted Catholic clericalism and its supernatural dogmas (although also saying he preferred it to political radicalism as a lesser evil). On the left, he fought the liberals and their naturalistic relativism. He also differed from those liberals who stressed social change instead of change of heart; the same issue had divided Coleridgeans from Benthamites one hundred years earlier. Babbitt's conserving of values was individualist and Protestant in temperament. He reinforced his favorite doctrine, the ethical "inner check," by translating Buddhist classics on that theme. Nearer home, he reinforced that doctrine via Burke, especially the Burke who wrote: "Society cannot exist unless a controlling power upon will and appetite be placed somewhere; and the less of it there is within, the more of it there must be without." Equally conservative, New England, and Protestant in spirit was Babbitt's thesis that Americans must learn to talk less of their rights, more of their duties.

Eliot vs. Babbitt. How much does conservatism depend upon religious dogma? That question emerged in the dramatic controversy between T. S. Eliot (1888-   ) and Irving Babbitt on whether their shared conservative ideals could be enforced without a supernatural religious backing. In his essay "The Humanism of Irving Babbitt," 1927, Eliot attacked Babbitt's classical humanism as lacking any solid sanction in religious dogma. Babbitt retorted (*On Being Creative*, 1932, pp. xxii, 260-261) by defining the "inner check" as ethical but nonsupernatural. Both sides of the Eliot-Babbitt debate (not reprinted in Part II because of copyright limitations but available in college libraries) represented the highest intellectual level of conservatism. The moderate, humanistic Babbitt was in the Burke tradition. The more clerical Eliot was in the Maistre tradition. In 1927 Eliot somewhat self-consciously informed mankind that he was "Anglo-Catholic in religion, royalist in politics, and classicist in literature." By 1948 he had become a Nobel Prize winner and the most influential and most pontifical poet of his time. With a Newman-style combination of sensitivity and dignity, his prose books advocated social and religious conservatism: *The Idea of a Christian Society,* 1940; *Notes Towards the Definition of Culture,* 1949.

Santayana on Liberalism. Throughout these pages, serious contradictions and inner conflicts have been noted in the conservative philosophy. Meanwhile, however, rigorous analysis by philosophers like George Santayana (1863-1952) maintains that the camp of liberal progress is riddled with contradictions even more self-destructive. In *Dominations and Powers,* 1951, Santayana pointed out the paradoxical consequences of idealistic nineteenth-century liberalism: it either ended in twentieth-century anarchy or, to avoid anarchy, imposed its will on an unliberal world. But by imposing its will, it ceased to be liberal, became despotic. Because of these equally deadly alternatives, Santayana pronounced the history of liberalism "virtually closed." (*See Document 29.*)

Southern Agrarians. Steeped in Eliot, More, and Babbitt, but more sectional, is the contemporary school of Southern agrarians: Donald Davidson, John Crowe Ransom, Allen Tate, Robert Penn Warren, and Richard Weaver. Their most influential manifesto was the symposium *I Take My Stand,* 1930. There the poet-philosopher Ransom (1888-   ) cited Ruskin and Carlyle on capitalist mechanization and hucksterism as a menace to traditional aristocratic and ethical values. Finding the Republican party too industrial, Ransom urged conservatives to rally to the Democratic party, provided it accepted three principles: "agrarian, conservative, anti-industrial."

Retort by Yankee Businessmen. Conversely, many wise and patriotic businessmen in the North, backed in all elections since 1936 by a majority of the press and finance of America, have rallied to the Republican party as a conservative bulwark against the Democratic party's "radical subversion" of *laisser-faire* economics. Good men are found on both these sides. They seem to be talking past each other with no shared terminology for defining which is the radical, which the conservative. Perhaps in reality they are neither. Perhaps both are merely variations of the same liberal philosophy of John Locke, the middle-road British philosopher, whose defense of the parliamentary system of 1688 has equally influenced America's seeming left and seeming right. This hypothesis—that American parties have always been the same moderate Lockean "liberals" at heart—has been given weight by the latest research of Louis Hartz, *The Liberal Tradition in America,* 1955.

Our Parties Nonideological. On the other hand, other scholars of equal persuasiveness believe that the word "liberal" lost all descriptive meaning during its overuse in the days when both parties claimed it. More recently, the word "conservative" became equally meaningless when—simultaneously—President Dwight D. Eisenhower labeled his Republican creed "progressive conservatism" (1955) while his Democratic rival of 1952, Adlai Stevenson, suggested: "The strange alchemy of time has somehow converted the Democrats into the truly conservative party of this country . . . building solidly and safely on [*traditional*] foundations. The Republicans, by contrast, are behaving like the radical party

—the party of the reckless. . . ." But this Republican-Democratic dispute, no matter which side you take, is irrelevant to conservatism, say those who see our party system as nonideological. In contrast with Europe, where ideological parties do exist, American parties tend to be temporary alliances of interest-groups, cutting across lines of conservative or anti-conservative with sublime indifference. Thereby they avoid those doctrinaire, inflexible collisions that sometimes reduce European politics to chaos and revolution. According to many authorities, the Federalists during 1787-1800 were America's only party of philosophical conservatism. Others aver that Burkean conservatism has tacitly taken over all our parties equally ever since. Solution: both viewpoints may be reconciled by calling all our post-Federalist parties liberal democrats in conscious theory, Burkean conservatives in unconscious practice.

Contemporary "New Conservatives." The young American scholars known as "New Conservatives" include John Blum, Daniel Boorstin, McGeorge Bundy, Thomas Cook, Raymond English, John Hallowell, Anthony Harrigan, August Heckscher, Milton Hindus, Russell Kirk, Klemens von Klemperer, Erik von Kuehnelt-Leddihn (not American but publishing here), Richard Leopold, S. A. Lukacs, Malcolm Moos, Robert Nisbet, Clinton Rossiter, Peter Viereck, Eliseo Vivas, Geoffrey Wagner, Chad Walsh, Francis Wilson. Their movement is too recent for analysis here; any reader interested may consult their books directly in the libraries. Among writers more famous and somewhat older than these, the following are generally Burkean in approach: Herbert Agar, Canon Bernard Bell, Gordon Keith Chalmers, Grenville Clark, Peter Drucker, Will Herberg (synthesizing Judaism with the new conservatism), Ross Hoffman (synthesizing Catholicism with Burke), and the perceptive commentators, Walter Lippmann and Dorothy Thompson. The Protestant theologian Reinhold Niebuhr, America's outstanding Burkean critic of liberal illusions about human nature, is claimed by philosophical conservatives and political liberals alike.

The foregoing contemporary Americans differ from each other. Yet all are Burkean. They agree with the New Conservative Thomas Cook that liberty depends on concrete traditions and is menaced by "excessive reliance on human reason, functioning deductively and *a priori* on a foundation of abstract principle." Stanley Pargellis, another gifted contemporary, adds: "The rationalist or the liberal frames his political decisions in accordance with some theory derived from an abstract notion of universal truth; the conservative takes into consideration an extremely wide variety of [*concrete*] acts. . . ." Reading these two New Conservative quotations, one seems to be attending all over again the debate between Burke and the rationalist liberal, Paine.

Relevance of Burke-Paine Debate Today. To many semi-Marxist intellectuals of the 1930's, the ghost of Burke was a pariah. Had not Marx himself damned Burke forever for slandering the French Revolution? But in the "cold war" of the 1950's, after American disillusionment with radical utopias, Burke was as eagerly studied by anti-communists as he once had been by anti-Jacobins. Crane Brinton, no conservative but a distinguished liberal historian, has summarized what the Burke-Paine debate may mean for America today (*The New York Times Book Review,* March 6, 1949):

"Burke confronted in the French Revolution the kind of challenge we have confronted and still confront in the totalitarian revolutions of our day. He met that challenge by an appeal to the fundamental standards of our Western civilization, an appeal which has itself helped clarify and formulate those standards. The debate between Burke and Paine, whose famous 'Rights of Man' was a pamphlet in reply to Burke's 'Reflections on the French Revolution,' has been decided in favor of Burke as clearly as the debate over the relation between the motions of sun and earth has been decided in favor of Copernicus. . . . Anyone brought up in the Christian tradition should from the start be proof against the great error Burke spent his life combating, namely, that human beings are born naturally good and naturally reasonable."

PART II

DOCUMENTS[1]

[1] The order is chronological. When several documents appear for the same year, the order within that year is alphabetical. When documents of varying dates appear under the same author, his chronological order is determined by the first document listed under him. Ordinarily the documents are dated by their dates of publication. But where publication followed writing by an unusual interval (for example, J. Q. Adams), the date of writing is used instead. References in Part I to these documents are by number only.

— Document 1 —

EDMUND BURKE: [A] *THOUGHTS,* 1770[1]

To show that an embryonic form of his later conserv-
ative philosophy was already stirring in Burke's mind
before the French Revolution, here is a paragraph dated
1770. It curiously anticipates the arguments he was to
use against that Revolution in his Reflections.

↗   ↗   ↗

Nations are not primarily ruled by laws. . . . Nations
are governed by the same methods and on the same principles by which an individual without authority is often
able to govern those who are his equals or his superiors;
by a knowledge of their temper and by a judicious man-
agement of it. . . . The laws reach but a very little way.
Constitute government how you please, infinitely the
greater part of it must depend upon the exercise of the
powers which are left at large to the prudence and
uprightness of ministers of state. Even all the use and
potency of the laws depend upon them. Without them,
your commonwealth is no better than a scheme upon
paper; not a living, active, effective constitution.

[B] *REFLECTIONS ON THE REVOLU-*
TION IN FRANCE, 1790[2]

This is the most important single document in the
philosophy of conservatism. Anyone seriously interested
in conservatism will read Reflections *in its entirety, which*
present space limits forbid. Such a reading will also show
how much all the other conservatives here quoted have

[1] Edmund Burke, *Thoughts on the Causes of the Present Dis-*
   contents, London, 1770.
[2] Edmund Burke, *Works,* 8 vols., Boston, Wells and Lilly,
   1826 ff.; III, *passim.*

borrowed from Burke. The excerpts here chosen were picked to emphasize his contrast between liberty with historical roots and "liberty in the abstract."

✓ ✓ ✓

Is it because liberty in the abstract may be classed amongst the blessings of mankind that I am seriously to felicitate a madman, who has escaped from the protecting restraint and wholesome darkness of his cell, on his restoration to the enjoyment of light and liberty? . . . I should therefore suspend my congratulations on the new liberty of France, until I was informed how it had been combined with government. . . . The effect of liberty to individuals is, that they may do what they please; we ought to see what it will please them to do, before we risk congratulations, which may be soon turned into complaints. . . . The French Revolution is the most astonishing that has hitherto happened in the world. . . . Everything seems out of nature in this strange chaos of levity and ferocity. . . . It cannot, however, be denied, that to some this strange scene . . . inspired no other sentiments than those of exultation and rapture. . . .

You will observe that, from Magna Carta to the Declaration of Right, it has been the uniform policy of our constitution to claim and assert our liberties, as an entailed inheritance derived to us from our forefathers, and to be transmitted to our posterity; as an estate specially belonging to the people of this kingdom; without any reference whatever to any other more general or prior right. By this means our constitution preserves a unity in so great a diversity of its parts. We have an inheritable crown; an inheritable peerage; and a House of Commons and a people inheriting privileges, franchises, and liberties, from a long line of ancestors. . . . Inheritance furnishes a sure principle of conservation and a sure principle of transmission; without at all excluding a principle of improvement. It leaves acquisition free; but it secures what it acquires. . . . In this choice of inheritance we have given to our frame of polity the image of a relation in blood; binding up the constitution of our country with our dearest domestic ties; adopting our fundamental laws into the bosom of our family affections; keeping inseparable, and cherishing with the warmth of all their combined and mutually reflected charities, our state, our hearths, our sepulchers, and our altars. . . .

We procure reverence to our civil institutions on the principle upon which nature teaches us to revere individual men; on account of their age, and on account of those from whom they are descended. All your sophisters cannot produce anything better adapted to preserve a rational and manly freedom than the course that we have pursued, who have chosen our nature rather than our speculations, our breasts rather than our inventions, for the great conservatories and magazines of our rights and privileges. . . . After I had read over the list of the persons and descriptions selected into the *Tiers État*, nothing which they afterwards did could appear astonishing. Among them, indeed, I saw some of known rank; some of shining talents; but of any practical experience in the state, not one man was to be found. . . . When the National Assembly has completed its work, it will have accomplished its ruin. . . . The person, whom they persevere in calling their king, has not power left to him by the hundredth part sufficient to hold together this collection of republics. . . .

It is no wonder, therefore, that with these ideas of everything in their constitution and government at home, either in church or state, as illegitimate and usurped or at best as a vain mockery, they look abroad with an eager and passionate enthusiasm. Whilst they are possessed by these notions, it is vain to talk to them of the practice of their ancestors, the fundamental laws of their country, the fixed form of a constitution, whose merits are confirmed by the solid test of long experience, and an increasing public strength and national prosperity. They despise experience as the wisdom of unlettered men; and as for the rest, they have wrought under ground a mine that will blow up, at one grand explosion, all examples of antiquity, all precedents, charters, and acts of parliament. They have "the rights of men." Against these there can be no prescription; against these no agreement is binding; these admit no temperament and no compromise: anything withheld from their full demand is so much of fraud and injustice. Against these their rights of men let no government look for security. . . .

Far am I from denying . . . the *real* rights of men. In denying their false claims of right, I do not mean to injure those which are real, and are such as their pretended rights would totally destroy. . . . Whatever each man can separately do, without trespassing upon others, he has a right to do for himself. . . .

Government is not made in virtue of natural rights, which may and do exist in total independence of it; and exist in much greater clearness, and in a much greater degree of abstract perfection: but their abstract perfection is their practical defect. By having a right to everything they want everything. Government is a contrivance of human wisdom to provide for human wants. Men have a right that these wants should be provided for by this wisdom. Among these wants is to be reckoned the want, out of civil society, of a sufficient restraint upon their passions. . . . This can only be done by a power out of themselves: and not, in the exercise of its function, subject to that will and to those passions which it is its office to bridle and subdue. In this sense the restraints on men, as well as their liberties, are to be reckoned among their rights. . . . This it is which makes the constitution of a state, and the due distribution of its powers, a matter of the most delicate and complicated skill. It requires a deep knowledge of human nature. . . . What is the use of discussing a man's abstract right to food or medicine? The question is upon the method of procuring and administering them. In that deliberation I shall always advise to call in the aid of the farmer and the physician, rather than the professor of metaphysics. . . .

The science of constructing a commonwealth, or renovating it, or reforming it, is, like every other experimental science, not to be taught *a priori*. . . . The science of government being therefore so practical in itself, and intended for such practical purposes, a matter which requires experience, and even more experience than any person can gain in his whole life, however sagacious and observing he may be, it is with infinite caution that any man ought to venture upon pulling down an edifice, which has answered in any tolerable degree for ages the common purposes of society. . . .

But now all is to be changed. All the pleasing illusions, which made power gentle and obedience liberal, which harmonized the different shades of life, and which, by a bland assimilation, incorporated into politics the sentiments which beautify and soften private society, are to be dissolved by this new conquering empire of light and

reason. All the decent drapery of life is to be rudely
torn off. All the superadded ideas, furnished from the
wardrobe of a moral imagination, which the heart owns,
and the understanding ratifies, as necessary to cover the
defects of our naked, shivering nature, and to raise it to
dignity in our own estimation, are to be exploded as a
ridiculous, absurd, and antiquated fashion. . . .

On this scheme of things, a king is but a man, a queen
is but a woman; a woman is but an animal, and an
animal not of the highest order. . . . On the scheme
of this barbarous philosophy, which is the offspring of
cold hearts and muddy understandings, and which is
as void of solid wisdom as it is destitute of all taste and
elegance, laws are to be supported only by their own
terrors, and by the concern which each individual may
find in them from his own private speculations, or can
spare to them from his own private interests. In the
groves of their academy, at the end of every vista, you
see nothing but the gallows. . . .

Society is indeed a contract. Subordinate contracts for
objects of mere occasional interest may be dissolved at
pleasure—but the state ought not to be considered as
nothing better than a partnership agreement in a trade
of pepper and coffee, calico or tobacco, or some other
such low concern, to be taken up for a little temporary
interest, and to be dissolved by the fancy of the parties.
It is to be looked on with other reverence; because it is
not a partnership in things subservient only to the gross
animal existence of a temporary and perishable nature.
It is a partnership in all science; a partnership in all art;
a partnership in every virtue, and in all perfection. As the
ends of such a partnership cannot be obtained in many
generations, it becomes a partnership not only between
those who are living, but between those who are living,
those who are dead, and those who are to be born.

Each contract of each particular state is but a clause
in the great primeval contract of eternal society, linking
the lower with the higher natures, connecting the visible
and invisible world, according to a fixed compact sanctioned by the inviolable oath which holds all physical
and all moral natures, each in their appointed place.
This law is not subject to the will of those, who by an
obligation above them, and infinitely superior, are bound
to submit their will to that law. . . . But if . . . the

law is broken, nature is disobeyed, and the rebellious
are outlawed, cast forth, and exiled from this world
of reason, and order, and peace, and virtue, and fruitful penitence, into the antagonist world of madness, discord, vice, confusion, and unavailing sorrow.

— Document 2 —

JOHN ADAMS: *APHORISMS,* 1776-1821 [3]

*Of all American presidents, John Adams best embodied
Burke-style conservatism: liberty-loving and anti-reactionary. These scattered aphorisms are here excerpted from
varied essays and letters of a lifetime. Note his conservative attacks on Paine, Rousseau, and abstract democratic
doctrinaires. Note his defense of inequality, natural aristocracy, and division of powers. Contrast with Calhoun
(Document 13)* the concluding passage on slavery, re-
minding us that American conservatives were found on
both sides of the issue.

✓ ✓ ✓

. . . The judicial power ought to be distinct from
both the legislative and executive, and independent upon
both, that so it may be a check upon both, as both
should be checks upon that. [*1776*]
. . . There are inequalities . . . which no human
legislator ever can eradicate . . . because they have a
natural and inevitable influence in society. . . . Some
individuals, whether by descent from their ancestors,
or from greater skill, industry, and success in business,
have estates both in lands and goods of great value.

[3] *Works of John Adams,* ed. by C. F. Adams, 10 vols., Boston,
1850-1856; IV, 193-200, 379-382 (and *passim* from *Defense of the Constitutions*); VI, 414-420, 427-431, 519-
521; IX, 616-618, 627, 635-640; X, 10-13, 210-213, 256,
379-380. *Statesman and Friend, Correspondence of John
Adams with Benjamin Waterhouse,* ed. by W. C. Ford,
Boston, Little, Brown Co., 1927; pp. 122-125, 155-158.

. . . Men of letters, men of the learned professions, and others, from acquaintance, conversation, and civilities, will be connected with them. . . . Among the wisest people that live, there is a degree of admiration, abstracted from all dependence, obligation, expectation, or even acquaintance, which accompanies splendid wealth. . . . Children of illustrious families have generally greater advantages of education. . . . The characters of their ancestors described in history, or coming down by tradition, removes them farther from vulgar jealousy. . . . Will any man pretend that the name of Andros and that of Winthrop are heard with the same sensations in any village of New England? . . . [There] the office of justice of the peace and even the place of representative, which has ever depended only on the freest election of the people, have generally descended from generation to generation in three or four families at most. . . . Honor, affection, and gratitude are due from children to those who gave them birth, nurture, and education. [From Defense of the Constitutions, 1787-1788.]

Governments are divided into despotisms, monarchies, and republics. A despotism is a government in which the three divisions of power, the legislative, executive, and judicial, are all vested in one man. . . . Let us now consider what our constitution is, and see whether any other name can with propriety be given it than that of a monarchical republic, or, if you will, a limited monarchy. The duration of our president is neither perpetual nor for life; it is only for four years; but his power during those four years is much greater than that of . . . a king of Poland; nay, than a king of Sparta. [1789]

The nobles have been essential parties in the preservation of liberty . . . against kings and people. . . . By nobles, I mean not peculiarly an hereditary nobility, or any particular modification, but the natural and actual aristocracy among mankind. The existence of this you will not deny. You and I have seen four noble families rise up in Boston. . . . Blind, undistinguishing reproaches against the aristocratical part of mankind, a division which nature has made and we cannot abolish, are neither pious nor benevolent. . . . It would not be true, but it would not be more egregiously false, to say that the people have waged everlasting war against the rights of men.

. . . The numbers of men in all ages have preferred ease, slumber, and good cheer to liberty. . . . We must not, then, depend alone upon the love of liberty in the soul of man for its preservation. Some political institutions must be prepared, to assist this love against its enemies. . . . When the people who have no property feel the power in their own hands to determine all questions by a majority, they ever attack those who have property. . . . The multitude, therefore, as well as the nobles, must have a check. [*1790*]

Paine's wrath was excited because my plan of government was essentially different from the silly projects that he had published in his *Common Sense*. By this means I became suspected and unpopular with the leading demagogues. . . . His political writings, I am singular enough to believe, have done more harm than his irreligious ones. He understood neither government nor religion. From a malignant heart he wrote virulent declamations, which the enthusiastic fury of the times intimidated all men, even Mr. Burke, from answering as he ought. . . . His billingsgate . . . will never discredit Christianity, which will hold its ground in some degree as long as human nature shall have anything moral or intellectual left in it. . . . Religion and virtue are the only foundations, not only of republicanism and of all free government, but of social felicity under all governments. . . . Mr. Jefferson speaks of my political opinions; but I know of no difference between him and myself relative to the Constitution. . . . We differed in opinion about the French Revolution. He thought it wise and good, and that it would end in the establishment of a free republic. I saw through it, to the end of it, before it broke out, and was sure it could end only in a restoration of the Bourbons, or a military despotism, after deluging France and Europe in blood. [*Letters to Benjamin Rush, 1809-1811*.]

. . . There will always be giants as well as pygmies . . . the former will be aristocrats, the latter democrats, if not Jacobins. . . . [*1814*]

I never could understand the doctrine of the perfectibility of the human mind. . . . Despotism, or unlimited sovereignty, or absolute power is the same in a majority of a popular assembly, an aristocratical council, an oligarchical junto, and a single emperor. Equally arbitrary,

cruel, bloody, and in every respect diabolical. . . .
No man is more sensible than I am of the service to
science . . . and liberty that would have been rendered
by the encyclopedists and economists, by Voltaire,
D'Alembert, Buffon, Diderot, Rousseau, La Lande, Frederic and Catherine, if they had possessed common sense.
But they were all totally destitute of it. . . . They seemed
to believe that whole nations and continents had been
changed in their principles, opinions, habits, and feelings
by the sovereign grace of their almighty philosophy.
. . . They had not considered the force of early education
on the minds of millions. . . . [*Letters to Jefferson,
1814-1816.*]

I am not however of Rousseau's opinion. His notions
of the purity of morals in savage nations and the earliest
ages of civilized nations are mere chimeras. . . . Helvetius and Rousseau preached to the French nation
liberty, till they made them the most mechanical slaves;
equality till they destroyed all equity; *humanity* till they
became weasels and African panthers; and *fraternity* till
they cut one another's throats like Roman gladiators.
[*1817, 1821*]

. . . The turpitude, the inhumanity, the cruelty, and
the infamy of the African commerce in slaves have been
so impressively represented . . . that nothing I can say
would increase the just odium in which it is and ought
to be held. Every measure of prudence, therefore, ought
to be assumed for the eventual total extirpation of slavery
from the United States. [*1819*]

— Document 3 —

ALEXANDER HAMILTON: *THE FEDERALIST*, NO. 9, 1787 [4]

[4] *Independent Journal,* November 21, 1787. Reprinted in
Alexander Hamilton, John Jay, and James Madison, *The
Federalist,* Philadelphia, 1892; and countless subsequent
editions.

*More centralizing than more typical conservatives,
Hamilton defended strengthening the newborn American
government on the conservative ground of preventing
"the rapid succession of revolutions" and "guarding internal tranquility." Contrast this with the decentralizing
conservatism of Calhoun* (Document 13).

A firm Union will be of the utmost moment to the
peace and liberty of the States, as a barrier against domestic faction and insurrection. It is imposisble to read
the history of the petty republics of Greece and Italy
without feeling sensations of horror and disgust at the
distractions with which they were continually agitated,
and at the rapid succession of revolutions by which they
were kept in a state of perpetual vibration between the
extremes of tyranny and anarchy. . . . The regular distribution of power into distinct departments; the introduction of legislative balances and checks; the institution of courts composed of judges holding their offices
during good behavior; the representation of the people
in the legislature by deputies of their own election . . .
tend to the amelioration of popular systems of civil
government; . . . [*so does*] ENLARGEMENT of the
ORBIT within which such systems are to revolve, either
in respect to the dimensions of a single State, or to the
consolidation of several smaller States into one great
Confederacy. . . .

The utility of a Confederacy, as well to suppress faction and to guard the internal tranquility of States, as to
increase their external force and security, is in reality
not a new idea. It has been practiced upon in different
countries and ages, and has received the sanction of the
most approved writers on the subjects of politics. . . .

The proposed Constitution, so far from implying an
abolition of the State governments, makes them constituent parts of the national sovereignty, by allowing them
a direct representation in the Senate, and leaves in their
possession certain exclusive and very important portions
of sovereign power. This fully corresponds, in every
rational import of the terms, with the idea of a federal
government.

— Document 4 —

JAMES MADISON: *THE FEDERALIST,* NO. 10, 1787[5]

Madison's typically "Federalist Paper" warning against "pure democracy" and his distinction "between a democracy and a republic" have remained basic for American conservatives and anti-majoritarians ever since. See Calhoun on "concurrent majority" and Babbitt on "indirect democracy" (Documents 13 and 27).

Among the numerous advantages promised by a well-constructed union, none deserves to be more accurately developed than its tendency to break and control the violence of faction. . . . By a faction, I understand a number of citizens, whether amounting to a majority or minority of the whole, who are united and actuated by some common impulse of passion, or of interest, adverse to the rights of other citizens or to the permanent and aggregate interests of the community. . . . If a faction consists of less than a majority, relief is supplied by the republican principle, which enables the majority to defeat its sinister views by regular vote. It may clog the administration, it may convulse the society; but it will be unable to execute and mask its violence under the forms of the Constitution. When a majority is included in a faction, the form of popular government, on the other hand, enables it to sacrifice to its ruling passion or interest both the public good and the rights of other citizens. To secure the public good, and private rights, against the danger of such a faction, and at the same time to preserve the spirit and the form of popular government, is then the great object to which our inquiries are directed. . . . Either the existence of the same passion or interest in a majority, at the same time, must be prevented; or the majority, having such co-

[5] *The Federalist,* Philadelphia, 1892; pp. 104-112. In the *N.Y. Daily Advertiser,* November 22, 1787.

existent passion or interest, must be rendered, by their number and local situation, unable to concert and carry into effect schemes of oppression. . . .

A pure democracy, by which I mean a society consisting of a small number of citizens, who assemble and administer the government in person, can admit of no cure for the mischiefs of faction. A common passion or interest will, in almost every case, be felt by a majority of the whole; a communication and concert results from the form of government itself; and there is nothing to check the inducements to sacrifice the weaker party or an obnoxious individual. Hence it is that such democracies have ever been spectacles of turbulence and contention; have ever been found incompatible with personal security, or the rights of property, and have in general been as short in their lives as they have been violent in their deaths. Theoretic politicians, who have patronized this species of government, have erroneously supposed that by reducing mankind to a perfect equality in their political rights, they would at the same time be perfectly equalized and assimilated in their possessions, their opinions, and their passions.

A republic, by which I mean a government in which the scheme of representation takes place, opens a different prospect, and promises the cure for which we are seeking. Let us examine the points in which it varies from pure democracy, and we shall comprehend both the nature of the cure and the efficacy which it must derive from the union.

The two great points of difference between a democracy and a republic are: First, the delegation of the government, in the latter, to a small number of citizens elected by the rest; secondly, the greater number of citizens, and greater sphere of country, over which the latter may be extended.

The effect of the first difference is, on the one hand, to refine and enlarge the public views, by passing them through the medium of a chosen body of citizens, whose wisdom may best discern the true interest of their country, and whose patriotism and love of justice will be least likely to sacrifice it to temporary or partial considerations. Under such a regulation, it may well happen that the public voice, pronounced by the representatives of the people, will be more consonant to the public good than if pronounced by the people themselves, convened for the purpose. . . .

The other point of difference is, the greater number of citizens and extent of territory which may be brought within the compass of republican than of democratic government; and it is this circumstance principally which renders factious combinations less to be dreaded in the former, than in the latter. . . . Extend the sphere, and you take in a greater variety of parties and interests; you make it less probable that a majority of the whole will have a common motive to invade the rights of other citizens. . . . Hence it clearly appears that the same advantage which a republic has over a democracy, in controlling the effects of faction, is enjoyed by a large over a small republic—is enjoyed by the Union over the States composing it . . . in the greater obstacles opposed to the concert and accomplishment of the secret wishes of an unjust and interested majority. . . . In the extent and proper structure of the Union, therefore, we behold a republican remedy for the diseases most incident to republican government.

— Document 5 —

JOHN QUINCY ADAMS: [A] LETTERS OF PUBLICOLA, 1791 [6]

Here is the important American counterpart of the debate between Burke and Paine. These unsigned articles by the son of John Adams rebutted Paine's radical Rights of Man *and defended constitutional restrictions on majorities.*

[6] Series in the newspaper *Columbian Centinel,* beginning June 8, 1791. (Reprinted in more available sources, including his *Writings,* 7 vols., ed. by W. C. Ford, New York, Macmillan, 1913-1917; I, 65-73.)

ⅳ   ⅳ   ⅳ

. . . Two pamphlets, founded upon very different
principles, appear to have been received with the greatest avidity . . . the one written by Mr. Burke . . . the
other the production of Mr. Paine, containing a defense
of the [*French Revolutionary*] Assembly. . . . Does he
[*Thomas Jefferson, who sponsored its publication*] consider this pamphlet of Mr. Paine's as the canonical book
of political scripture? . . .

[*Paine's*] intention appears evidently to be to convince
the people of Great Britain that they have neither
Liberty nor a Constitution—that their only possible means
to produce these blessings to themselves is to "topple
down headlong" their present government, and follow
implicitly the example of the French. As to the right, he
scruples not to say, "that which a whole nation chooses
to do, it has a right to do." This proposition is a part
of what Mr. Paine calls a system of principles in opposition to those of Mr. Burke. . . . This principle, that a
whole nation has a right to do whatever it pleases, cannot
in any sense whatever be admitted as true. The eternal
and immutable laws of justice and of morality are paramount to all human legislation. The violation of those
laws is certainly within the power, but it is not among the
rights of nations. . . . It is of infinite consequence that
the distinction between *power* and *right* should be fully
acknowledged, and admitted as one of the fundamental
principles of legislators. . . . If a majority . . . are
bound by no law human or divine, and have no other
rule but their sovereign will and pleasure to direct them,
what possible security can any citizen of the nation have
for the protection of his unalienable rights? The principles
of liberty must still be the sport of arbitrary power, and
the hideous form of despotism must lay aside the diadem
and the scepter, only to assume the party-colored gar-
ments of democracy. . . .

Mr. Paine has departed altogether from the principles
of the Revolution, and has torn up by the roots all reasoning from the British Constitution. . . . The right of a
people to legislate for succeeding generations derives all
its authority from the consent of that posterity who are
bound by their laws; and therefore the expressions of

perpetuity used by the Parliament of 1688 contain no absurdity; and expressions of a similar nature may be found in all the Constitutions of the United States. . . . So far as the principles of the English Constitution have been adopted by the Americans, I have defended them, and I am firmly convinced that we cannot renounce them without renouncing at the same time the happy governments with which we are favored.

[B] PARTIES IN THE UNITED STATES, CIRCA 1822 [7]

The son of Federalist John Adams describes what has been called America's "only conservative party," the Federalists.

✓   ✓   ✓

The merit of effecting the establishment of the Constitution of the United States belongs to the party called Federalists—the party favorable to the concentration of power in the federal head. The purposes for which the exercise of this power was necessary were principally the protection of property, and thereby the Federal Party became identified with the aristocratic part of the community. The principles of Federalism and aristocracy were thus blended together in the political system of the Federalists, and gathered to them a great majority of the men of wealth and education throughout the Union. The anti-Federalists had always the advantage of *numbers*. Their principles, being those of democracy, were always favored by the majority of the people. . . . The remnants of the Tories of the Revolution generally sided with the Federalists . . . exposing the whole Federal Party to the odium and obloquy of those opinions. . . . The name of anti-Federalists . . . was soon afterwards changed, the party which had worn it having the address to assume that of Republicans, and sometimes of Democrats—appellations which had the advantages of recom-

[7] J. Q. Adams, *Parties in the United States,* New York, 1941; pp. 6-10, 119-125. Reprinted by permission of Greenberg, Publisher.

mending them to the special favor òf the people and at
the same time stigmatizing their adversaries by the impli-
cation that they were anti-republicans, monarchists and
aristocrats. . . .

The Federalists, however, retained their denomination,
the principal cause of which was that the series of papers
under that titie published to promote the establishment
of the Constitution, and writen by General Hamilton, Mr.
Madison, and Mr. Jay, had in a manner identified it
with the Constitution itself. . . . From the formation
of the American Union by the meeting of the first Congress in September 1774, until the establishment of the
Constitution of the United States in March 1789, the
collision of opinions was upon the foundation of the
social compact to be formed. Then the division of
parties as Whig and Tory was natural. [*But since then*]
. . . there has been continual revolution of opinions between the Federal and the Republican parties, and the
practice of both has been in frequent and flagrant violation of their proposed principles.

— Document 6 —

SAMUEL T. COLERIDGE: *APHORISMS*
1798-1832 [8]

*In these representative aphorisms, here selected for the
reader from many different volumes, the great poet
and cultural conservative defends organic against mechanical unity; inner religious "cultivation" against outer
material "civilization" or "government"; landed aristocrats against rootless shopkeepers.*

[8] S. T. Coleridge, excerpt (1) is from *Letters*, Boston,
1895; I, 241. (2): *Letters on the Spaniards*, 1810, reprinted in *Essays on His Own Times*, London, 1850. (3):
On The Constitution of the Church and State, London,
1830; chapters 5-6. (4): *Table Talk*, London, 1835; item
of December 18, 1831. (5): *Table Talk* of February 24,
1832. (6): *Table Talk* of April 29, 1832.

✓   ✓   ✓

(1) One good consequence which I expect from [*disillusionment with*] revolution is that individuals will see the necessity of individual effort; that they will act as good Christians, rather than as citizens and electors; and so by degrees will purge off . . . the error of attributing to governments a talismanic influence over our virtues and our happiness, as if governments were not rather effects than causes. [*1798*]

(2) . . . There is an individual spirit that breathes through a whole people, is participated in by all, though not by all alike; a spirit which gives a colour and character to their virtues and vices, so that the same actions . . . are yet not the same in a Spaniard as they would be in a Frenchman . . . [*1810*]

(3) The object of the two former estates of the realm, which conjointly form the State, was to reconcile the interests of permanence with those of progression—law with liberty. The object of the National Church, the third remaining estate of the realm, was to secure and improve that civilisation without which the nation could be neither permanent nor progressive. . . . THE CLERISY of the nation, or national church, in its primary acceptation and original intention, comprehended the learned of all denominations;—the sages and professors of the law and jurisprudence; of medicine and physiology; of music; of military and civil architecture; of the physical sciences; with the mathematical as the common organ of the preceding; in short, all the so-called liberal arts and sciences, the possession and application of which constitute the civilisation of a country, as well as the Theological. The last was, indeed, placed at the head of all; and of good right did it claim the precedence. . . . It had the precedency because under the name theology were comprised all the main aids, instruments, and materials of NATIONAL EDUCATION, . . . the shaping and informing spirit, which *educing,* i.e. eliciting, the latent *man* in all the natives of the soil, *trains them up* to be citizens of the country, free subjects of the realm. And lastly, because to divinity belong those fundamental truths which are the common groundwork of our civil and religious duties, not less indispensable to a right view of our temporal concerns than to a rational faith respecting

our immortal well-being. (Not without celestial observations can even terrestrial charts be accurately constructed.) . . . A nation can never be a too cultivated, but may easily become an over-civilised race. It is folly to think of making all, or the many, philosophers, or even men of science and systematic knowledge. But it is duty and wisdom to aim at making as many as possible soberly and steadily religious;—in as much as the morality which the state requires in its citizens for its own well-being and ideal immortality, and without reference to their spiritual interest as individuals, can only exist for the people in the form of religion. . . . In fine, Religion, true or false, is and ever has been the centre of gravity in a realm, to which all other things must and will accommodate themselves. [*1830*]

(4) The difference between an inorganic and an organic body lies in this: in the first—a sheaf of corn—the whole is nothing more than a collection of the individual parts or phenomena. In the second—a man—the whole is everything and the parts are nothing. A State is an idea intermediate between the two, the whole being a result from, and not a mere total of, the parts,—and yet not so merging the constituent parts in the result, but that the individual exists integrally within it. [*1831*]

(5) [*Coleridge is attacking Grey's reform bill of 1832, which extended the vote from the landed to the commercial classes.*] I could not help smiling, in reading the report of Lord Grey's speech in the House of Lords, the other night, when he asked Lord Wicklow whether he seriously believed that he, Lord Grey, or any of the ministers, intended to subvert the institutions of the country. Had I been in Lord Wicklow's place, I should have been tempted to answer this question something in the following way: ". . . You have destroyed the freedom of Parliament; you have done your best to shut the door of the House of Commons to the property, the birth, the rank, the wisdom of the people, and have flung it open to their passions and their follies. You have disfranchised the gentry, and the real patriotism of the nation, you have agitated and exasperated the mob, and thrown the balance of political power into the hands of that class [the shop-keepers] which, in all countries and in all ages, has been, is now, and ever will be, the least patriotic and the least conservative of any. . . ." [*1832*]

(6) I never said that the *vox populi* was, of course, the *vox dei*. It may be; but it may be, with equal probability, *a priori*, *vox diaboli*. That the voice of ten millions of men calling for the same thing is a spirit, I believe; but whether that be a spirit of Heaven or Hell, I can only know by trying the thing called for by the prescript of reason and God's will. [*1832*]

— Document 7 —

fRIEDRICH GENTZ: ON THE POLITICAL CONDITION OF EUROPE, 1801 [9]

Translator of Burke and chief intellectual aide of Metternich, Gentz represents the original internationalism of the conservative mind, in contrast with its post-1870 nationalism.

✦ ✦ ✦

Through their geographic position, through the uniformity of their customs, their laws, their needs, their way of life, and their culture, all the states of this continent form a great political league, which with some justification has been dubbed the *European Republic*. . . . The various members of this *League of Nations* are in such close and incessant mutual communion that none can be indifferent to any important change occurring in another. It is saying too little to say that they exist next to each other. If they are to subsist, they must subsist with each other and through each other. Upon this indispensable communion the whole European international law is founded . . .

[9] Translated by P. Viereck from Friedrich Gentz, *Von dem politischen Zustande von Europe*, Berlin, 1801, a short brochure. Italics added.

— Document 8 —

JOSEPH DE MAISTRE: [A] *ESSAY ON THE GENERATIVE PRINCIPLE OF POLITICAL CONSTITUTIONS,* 1810[10]

The contrast between the rigid, dogmatic Maistre and the more flexible, evolutionary Burke still divides conservatives into their two main wings. Maistre remains the less experienced, less balanced of the two but the more consistent and more brilliant logician.

✔   ✔   ✔

I. One of the grand errors of an age, which professed them all, was, to believe that a political constitution could be written and created *à priori;* whilst reason and experience unite in establishing, that a constitution is a Divine work, and that which is most fundamental, and most essentially constitutional, in the laws of a nation, is precisely what cannot be written.

II. It has been often supposed to be an excellent piece of pleasantry upon Frenchmen, to ask them *in what book the Salic law was written?* But Jérôme Bignon answered, very apropos, and probably without knowing the full truth of what he said, *that it was written IN the hearts of Frenchmen.* Let us suppose, in effect, that a law of so much importance existed only because it was written; it is certain that any authority whatsoever which may have written it, will have the right of annulling it; the law will not then have that character of sacredness and immutability which distinguishes laws truly constitutional. . . .

IX. The more we examine the influence of human agency in the formation of political constitutions, the

[10] *Introduction to Contemporary Civilization in the West,* prepared by the contemporary civilization staff of Columbia College, New York, 1946, II, 92–105. Reprinted by permission of Columbia University Press.

greater will be our conviction that it enters there only in a manner infinitely subordinate, or as a simple instrument; and I do not believe there remains the least doubt of the incontestable truth of the following propositions:—

1. That the fundamental principles of political constitutions exist before all written law.

2. That a constitutional law is, and can only be, the development or sanction of an unwritten pre-existing right.

3. That which is most essential, most intrinsically constitutional, and truly fundamental, is never written, and could not be, without endangering the state.

4. That the weakness and fragility of a constitution are actually in direct proportion to the multiplicity of written constitutional articles. . . .

XII. Let us now consider some one political constitution, that of England, for example. It certainly was not made *à priori*. Her Statesmen never assembled themselves together and said, *Let us create three powers, balancing them in such a manner, etc.* No one of them ever thought of such a thing. The Constitution is the work of circumstances, and the number of these is infinite. Roman laws, ecclesiastical laws, feudal laws; Saxon, Norman, and Dutch customs; the privileges, prejudices, and claims of all orders; wars, revolts, revolutions, the Conquest, Crusades; virtues of every kind, and all vices; knowledge of every sort, and all errors and passions;—all these elements, in short, acting together, and forming, by their admixture and reciprocal action, combinations multiplied by myriads of millions, have produced at length, after many centuries, the most complex unity and happy equilibrium of political powers that the world has ever seen. . . .

XXVIII. Everything brings us back to the general rule, —*man cannot create a constitution; and no legitimate constitution can be written.* The collection of fundamental laws, which must essentially constitute a civil or religious society, never has been written, and never will be, *à priori*. It is only when society finds itself already constituted, without being able to say how, that it is possible to make known, or explain, in writing, certain special articles; but in almost every case these declarations or explanations are the effect or cause of very great evils, and always cost the people more than they are worth. . . .

XL. . . . The celebrated Zanotti has said, *It is difficult to alter things for the better.* . . . All men have a consciousness of this truth, without being in a state to explain it to themselves. Hence that instinctive aversion, in every good mind, to innovations. The word *reform,* in itself, and previous to all examination, will be always suspected by wisdom, and the experience of every age justifies this sort of instinct. We know too well what has been the fruit of the most beautiful speculations of this kind. . . .

LXVII. Europe is guilty for having closed her eyes against these great truths; and it is because she is guilty, that she suffers. . . .

[B] *EVENING CONVERSATIONS IN ST. PETERSBURG, 1821* [11]

Here ottantottism carries its rigid, deductive logic so far as to demand "loving" a "terrible" God, an "unjust" prince. Cf. par. 2 with Kafka's Castle.

I wish to put a question. Suppose you lived under the laws of a prince, I do not say an evil prince, but only a severe and suspicious prince, who watches his subjects closely. Would you take the same liberties with him as with another and entirely different prince, who would be happy to know all his people free and who would ever fear to exercise his power lest he should be feared? Certainly not. Very well, the comparison is self-evident. The more terrible God appears to us, the more we must fear Him and the more our prayers must become ardent and indefatigable.

We know of God's existence with greater certainty than of His attributes; we know that He is before we know what He is; and we shall never fully know what He is. We find ourselves in a realm whose sovereign has proclaimed his laws once and forever. On the whole these laws seem wise and even kind; nevertheless some of them

[11] Count Joseph de Maistre, *Les Soirées de Saint Petersbourg,* 5th edition, Lyon, 1845, II, 128-172. Unfinished at author's death, 1821, and published only later.

(I assume it for the moment) appear hard and even un-just. In this situation I ask all those who are dissatisfied, what should be done? Leave the realm, perhaps? Impossible: the realm is everywhere and nothing is outside it. To complain, to sulk, to write against the sovereign? That would mean to be flogged or put to death. There is no better course than resignation and respect, I would even say love; for since we start with the supposition that the master exists and that we must serve him absolutely, is it not better to serve him, whatever his nature, with love than without it? . . .

But do you know whence comes this torrent of insolent doctrines which judge God without ceremony and ask him to account for his decrees? It comes from the large phalanx which is called "the intellectuals," a group whom we have not learned how to control in this century or to keep in their place—which is the second place. Formerly there were very few intellectuals, and only a fraction of these were impious. Today one sees nothing but intellectuals. They are a profession, a crowd, a whole people, and among them what was formerly an exception, which was bad enough, has become the rule. They have usurped a limitless influence from all sides. Yet if there is one thing certain in the world, it is, in my opinion, that it does not belong to science to lead men.

Nothing vital has been confided to science. One must have lost all sense to believe that God has charged the Academies with teaching us what He is and what we owe Him. The prelates, the noblemen, the high dignitaries of the state, are the true repositaries and guardians of the verities. It falls to them to teach the nations good and bad, truth and falsehood in the moral and spiritual order. Others have no right to reason about these things. The intellectuals have the natural sciences to amuse them: of what do they complain? Anybody who speaks or writes to deprive the people of a national dogma should be hanged as a thieving servant. Rousseau himself has agreed to that without imagining the consequences for himself. Why have we been so imprudent as to allow everyone to speak freely? That is what has destroyed us. The intellectuals all have a certain ferocious and rebellious pride which does not accommodate itself to anything. They hate without exception all the distinctions which they do not enjoy themselves. Every authority displeases them. They hate everything that is above them. Let them, and they will attack everything, even God because He is the Lord.

— Document 9 —

ADAM MÜLLER: *ON THE NECESSITY OF A THEOLOGICAL BASIS FOR ALL POLITICAL SCIENCE AND POLITICAL ECONOMY IN PARTICULAR, 1819*[12]

A disciple of Burke but far more authoritarian and anti-rational, Adam Müller represents the reaction of German romanticism against eighteenth-century French rationalism.

✔   ✔   ✔

On the best constitution. . . . The individual has overstepped the bounds of his own small constitution, his small state, the natural and God-given limits of his freedom and obedience. . . . Political discussions on the general form of the state are vain play, a futile luxury of arrogant reasons compared to the gravity of this higher question of the disintegration into which all domestic life, small states and members of the larger states, have fallen. . . . No trace will remain of the political castles in the air which our century has erected. . . . When all the wounds of our century have ceased bleeding and all the passions which blinded our judgment have become calm, the future will accept the convulsions of our days as the awakening of religion. The future will understand the clamorous calls for constitutionality which drowned out quiet political investigation; it will recognize

[12] *Introduction to Contemporary Civilization in the West,* prepared by the contemporary civilization staff of Columbia College, New York, Columbia University Press, 1946, II, 115-116.

that there was only one constitution of merit, the quest
for the first and only political constitution the world has
known, the Christian.

— Document 10 —

CLEMENS VON METTERNICH: [A] *CONFESSION OF FAITH*, 1820 [13]

*The Hapsburg Chancelor Metternich sent this personal
credo as a "secret memorandum" on December 15, 1820
to Tsar Alexander I in order to combat whatever remained of the latter's youthful flirtations with Jacobin
ideas. Note the blending of the Maistre and the Burke
kinds of conservatism throughout these extracts: far more
reactionary than British conservatives and yet more open-
minded, less doctrinaire than the French ultra-royalists,
whom Metternich dismissed as counter-revolutionary
"white Jacobins."*

Kings have to calculate the chances of their very existence in the immediate future; passions are let loose. . . .
Two elements alone remain in all their strength, and
never cease to exercise their indestructible influence with
equal power. These are the precepts of *morality,* religious
as well as social, and the necessities created by *locality.*
. . . Attempts to swerve from these bases . . . will lead
to a state of convulsion. . . . The progress of the human
mind has been extremely rapid in the course of the last
three centuries. This *progress, having been accelerated
more rapidly than the growth of wisdom* (the only coun-
terpoise to passions and to error), a revolution (prepared
by the false systems, the fatal errors into which many
of the most illustrious sovereigns of the last half of the
eighteenth century fell), has at last broken out. . . .

[13] Metternich, *Memoirs,* 5 vols., London, 1880; New York,
    1881; III, 458 ff. (Italics added to bring out key con-
    cepts.)

The evil which threatens to deprive [*society*] of the fruits of genuine civilization. . . . This it is which at the present day leads so many individuals astray, for it has become an almost universal sentiment. Religion, morality, legislation, economy, politics, administration, all have become common and accessible to everyone. Knowledge seems to come by inspiration; *experience has no value for the presumptuous* man; faith is nothing to him; he substitutes for it a pretended individual conviction and to arrive at this conviction dispenses with all inquiry and with all study; for these means appear too trivial to a mind which believes itself strong enough to embrace at one glance all questions and all facts. Laws have no value for him, because he has not contributed to make them, and it would be beneath a man of his parts to recognize the limits traced by rude and ignorant generations. Power resides in himself; why should he submit himself to that which was only useful for the man deprived of light and knowledge?

It is *principally the middle class* of society which this moral gangrene has affected, and it is only among them that the real heads of the party are found. For the great mass of the people it has no attraction. . . . The people know what is the happiest thing for them: namely, to be able to count on the morrow. . . . The governments, in establishing the principle of *stability*, will *in no wise exclude the development* of what is good, for *stability is not immobility*. . . . A league between all governments against factions in all states . . . union between the monarchs is the basis of the policy which must now be followed to save society from total ruin. . . .

The world desires to be governed by facts and according to justice, not by phrases and theories; the first need of society is to be maintained by strong authority (no authority without real strength deserves the name) and not to govern itself. In comparing the number of contests between parties in mixed governments, and that of just complaints caused by aberrations of power in a Christian state, the comparison would not be in favor of the new doctrines. The first and greatest concern for the immense majority of every nation is the stability of the laws, and their uninterrupted action—never their change. Therefore, let the governments govern. Let them maintain the groundwork of their institutions. . . . Let them maintain

religious principles in all their purity, and not allow
the faith to be attacked and morality interpreted according to the *social contract* or the visions of foolish secta-
rians. Let them *suppress secret societies,* that gangrene
of society. In short, let the great monarchs strengthen
their union . . . paternal and protective, menacing only
the disturbers of public tranquillity.

[B] *EPIGRAMS AGAINST EXTREMES*
OF RIGHT OR LEFT, 1817-1848[14]

*These characteristic epigrams, here brought together
for the first time from his many volumes of letters and
memoirs, may give a different picture than the nationalist
and liberal view of Metternich as a bigoted, black reactionary. They show him in such little-known roles as
fighting behind the scenes with his bigoted emperor
against thought-control and on behalf of constitutions for
the Italians and Hungarians and calling himself a "conservative socialist." The many sources within the long
footnote below are numbered separately so as to corre-
spond with the numbers prefixed to their respective
quotations, which follow.*

        ✓   ✓   ✓

    (1) The human mind generally revels in extremes. A
period of irreligion . . . has been necessarily followed
by . . . religious reaction. Now, every kind of reaction
is false and unjust. [*June, 1817*]

    (2) In 1815 [*Tsar Alexander*] abandoned pure Jacob-

[14] (1) Metternich, *Memoirs,* III, 58. (2) III, 62. (3) III, 102-
107. (4) III, 264. (5) III, 394-395. (6) IV, 159. (7)
Quoted in Srbik, *Metternich,* 2 vols., Munich, 1925; I,
71. (8) Quoted in Egon Friedell, *A Cultural History of
the Modern Age,* 3 vols., New York, 1931-1933; III, 25.
(9) *Memoirs,* IV, 200. (10) *Mémoires* (French edition),
VII, 402. (11) *Mémoires,* VIII, 175. (12) Srbik, II, 307.
Mémoires, VIII, 187. (13) *Mémoires,* VII, 640. *Memoirs,*
III, 366-367, 506. (14) *Memoirs,* III, 386. (15) *Memoirs,*
III, 367. Second sentence quoted in Viktor Bibl, *Metternich in Neuer Beleuchtung,* Vienna, 1928. (16) Metternich quoted in A. J. Huebner, *Une année de ma vie*
(1848-1849), Paris, 1891, pp. 15-21.

inism but only to throw himself into mysticism. [*August, 1817*]

(3) I think it my duty to repeat again, with the greatest respect, how important it would be, from a political point of view, to remove as soon as possible these defects and shortcomings in the most interesting part of the monarchy [*namely, Italy*], to quicken and advance the progress of business, to conciliate the national spirit and self-love of the nation by giving to these provinces a form of *constitution,* which might prove to the Italians that we have no desire to deal with them as with the German provinces of the monarchy, or, so to speak, to weld them with these provinces; that we should there appoint, especially in the magisterial offices, able natives of the country. [*Letter of November 1817 warning his emperor against antagonizing the Hapsburg possessions in Italy.*]

(4) My constant efforts are directed against ultras of all kinds.

(5) My life has fallen at a hateful time. I have come into the world either too early or too late. Now I do not feel comfortable; earlier, I should have enjoyed the time; later I should have helped to build it up again; today I have to give my life to prop up the moldering edifice. [*Letter of 1820 about his Hapsburg edifice.*]

(6) The red and white doctrinaires shun me like the plague. [*Letter from Paris, 1825.*]

(7) From the school of radicalism I fell into that of the émigrés and learned to value the mean between the extremes.

(8) The Legitimists are legitimatizing the Revolution. [*A sarcastic description of the extreme French Royalists.*]

(9) Certainly a democracy does not exist here [*Hungary*]; the struggle goes on between the pure Royalists and the friends of constitution. Since the Emperor Joseph II's accession to the throne, the government opposed the Constitution. I caused the Emperor to take a reversed position within the bounds of the Constitution. [*1825*]

(10) The true character of our time is that of an era of *transition.* Fate imposed on me the duty of coming between the phases of this era. . . . To me the political game did not at all seem to answer to the needs of the time; I made myself a conservative socialist [*socialiste conservateur*]. The conservative principles are applicable to the most diverse situations; their worship is not en-

closed within narrow bounds; they are enemies of anarchy, moral and material. [*Letter to French Premier Guizot, 1847.*]

(11) To ruin those who possess something is not to come to the aid of those who possess nothing; it is only to render misery general. [*Letter against the class-war kind of socialism.*]

(12) [*England is*] the freest land on earth *because* the best disciplined. . . . The English aristocracy is not the noblesse. It consists of the conservative principles . . . animating *all* classes.

(13) Man cannot make a constitution, properly speaking, [*only*] time. . . . The English constitution is the work of centuries. . . . There is no universal recipe for constitutions. . . . Madame de Stael would not find it difficult to show that the weather is bad because the English constitution is not introduced everywhere. [*1820, 1821, etc.*]

(14) A people who can neither read nor write, whose last word is the dagger—fine material for constitutional principles! [*Ironic comment of 1820 on liberal revolution in Naples.*]

(15) What is called a constitution nowadays is nothing but "get out so I can get in." . . . The first instrument in the hands of the middle class is the modern representative system. [*1820, 1831*]

(16) [*The Emperor Francis*] followed my advice in everything on foreign policy. He did not do so in internal affairs. . . . Attributing a perhaps exaggerated importance to the secret societies . . . he thought he found the remedy against the evil in a minute surveillance of the would-be intellectual classes exercised by the police, who thereby became one of the chief instruments of his governments; . . . in short, in a moral closing of the frontiers. . . . The result was a dull irritation against the government among the educated classes. I told that to the emperor; but on that point he was unshakable. All I could do to lessen the grievous results, I did. . . . If in 1817, even as late as 1826, the emperor had adopted my ideas on the reorganization of the diets, we would be perhaps in a position to face the tempest. Today it is too late. . . . It is useless to close the gates against ideas; they overleap them. . . . [*March 1, 1848, ironically only about two weeks before the revolution hit Vienna and overthrew Metternich.*]

— Document 11 —

BENJAMIN DISRAELI: [A] *VINDICA-TION OF THE ENGLISH CONSTITUTION,* 1835 [15]

Note here Disraeli's typically Tory "respect for prece-dent" and "antiquity." The additional documents were chosen to illustrate his simultaneous wooing of two anti-middle-class groups: the landowning aristocrat, the urban workingman.

This respect for precedent, this clinging to prescription, this reverence for antiquity, which are so often ridiculed by conceited and superficial minds, and move the special contempt of the gentlemen who admire abstract prin-ciples, appear to me to have their origin in a profound knowledge of human nature and in a fine observation of public affairs, and satisfactorily account for the perma-nent character of our liberties. Those great men who have periodically risen to guide the helm of our government in times of tumultuous and stormy exigency, knew that a state is a complicated creation of refined art, and they handled it with all the delicacy the exquisite machinery requires. They knew that if once they admitted the abstract rights of subjects, they must inevitably advance to the abstract rights of men, and then the very founda-tions of their civil polity would sink beneath them. . . . It is to this deference for what Lord Coke called reverend antiquity that I ascribe the duration of our common-wealth, and it is the spirit that has prevented even our revolutions from being destructive. . . .

I do not see, my Lord, that this reverence for antiquity has checked the progress of knowledge or stunted the growth of liberty in this island. We are universally held to be the freest people in Europe, and to have enjoyed

[15] Benjamin Disraeli, *Vindication of the English Constitution,* London, 1835.

our degree of freedom for a longer period than any existing state. . . . Assuredly this *summum bonum* is not
to be found ensconced behind a revolutionary barricade,
or floating in the bloody gutters of an incendiary metrop-
olis. It cannot be scribbled down—this great invention—
in a morning on the envelope of a letter by some char-
ter-concocting monarch, or sketched with ludicrous
facility in the conceited commonplace book of a Utilitarian sage. With us it has been the growth of ages, and
brooding centuries have watched over and tended its
perilous birth and feeble infancy.

[B] *ANTI-LIBERAL SPEECH FOR NA- TIONAL AGAINST SEPARATIST PRINCIPLES, 1847*[16]

In the great struggle between popular principles and
liberal opinions, which is the characteristic of our age,
I hope ever to be found on the side of the people, and of
the Institutions of England. . . . Liberal opinions are the
opinions of those who would be free from certain con-
straints and regulations, from a certain dependence and
duty which are deemed necessary for the general and
popular welfare. Liberal opinions are very convenient
opinions for the rich and the powerful. They ensure
enjoyment and are opposed to self-sacrifice. The holder
of Liberal opinions, for example, maintains that the
possession of land is to be considered in a commercial
light and no other. He looks to the income which it will
afford him. It is not a Liberal principle that the holder
of land should incur the duty of executing justice and
maintaining truth among the multitude for nothing. That,
gentlemen, is a popular principle, a principle of government for the benefit of the people, not a Liberal opinion.
A poor law is founded upon a popular principle: Liberal
opinions are entirely averse to its enactments.

[16] An address by Disraeli to the electors of Bucks County,
1847.

Instead of royalty, a gentleman of Liberal opinions would prefer that the supreme executive should be entrusted to a person of his own class, with the title of President, and perhaps to have the chance of becoming President himself; instead of a national Church he prefers to choose and pay for his own minister of religion, if he has a wish for one; and although he is not averse to the theory of representative government, provided the representation is absorbed by his own order, he encourages the real transaction of affairs to be conducted by paid commissioners and select committees.

[C] SPEECH IN DEFENSE OF LANDED ARISTOCRACY, MARCH, 1848[17]

Nothing is to be more deprecated, nothing is more dangerous, than that considerable classes of the country should deem that they are treated unfairly by the Legislature. Sir, the spirit of the landed interest is deeply wounded. . . .

I fancy, Sir, it has been somewhat too long the practice to believe that you might conduct yourselves toward the landed interest with impunity. It was even a proverb with Sir Robert Walpole that the landed interest might be fleeced at pleasure; and I observe at no time has that interest been more negligently treated than when demagogues are denouncing it as an oligarchical usurpation. But this may be dangerous play if you are outraging justice. You think you may trust their proverbial loyalty. Trust their loyalty, but do not abuse it. I dare say it may be said of them, as it was said 2,000 years ago, in the most precious legacy of political science that has descended to us . . . that the agricultural class is the least given to sedition. . . .

Your system and theirs are exactly contrary. They in-

[17] R. J. White, editor, The Conservative Tradition, London, Nicholas Kaye, 1950, pp. 193-194.

vite union. They believe that national prosperity can only be produced by the prosperity of all classes. You prefer to remain in isolated splendour and solitary magnificence. But believe me I speak not as your enemy when I say that it will be an exception to the principles which seem hitherto to have ruled society, if you can succeed in maintaining the success at which you aim without the possession of that permanence and stability which the territorial principle alone can afford.

[D] TWO SPEECHES ON THE NEED TO REDISCOVER TORY PRINCIPLES, 1862, 1863 [18]

✓   ✓   ✓

[From a speech in Parliament in 1862:]

Ever since that period of disaster and dismay, when my friends and myself were asked for the first time to sit upon these benches, it has ever been our habit, in counselling the Tory party, to recur gradually but most sincerely to the original elements of that great political connection. To build up a community, not upon Liberal opinions, which anyone may fashion to his fancy, but upon popular principles, which assert equal rights, civil and religious; to uphold the institutions of the country because they are the embodiments of the wants and wishes of the nation, and protect us alike from individual tyranny and popular outrage; equally to resist democracy and oligarchy, and favour that principle of free aristocracy which is the only basis and security for constitutional government; to be vigilant to guard and prompt to vindicate the honour of the country, but to hold aloof from that turbulent diplomacy which only distracts the mind of a people from internal improvement; to lighten taxation; frugally but wisely to administer the public treasure; to favour popular education, because it is the best guarantee for public order; to defend local

[18] Both quoted in W. F. Monypenny and G. E. Buckle, *Life of Disraeli*, 6 vols., London, 1910-1920, vol. IV, chap. 10.

government, and to be as jealous of the rights of the working man as of the prerogative of the Crown and the privileges of the senate—these were once the principles which regulated Tory statesmen, and I for one have no wish that the Tory party should ever be in power unless they practice them.

*   *   *

[*From a speech at a dinner-party in 1863:*]

The Tory party is only in its proper position when it represents popular principles. Then it is truly irresistible. Then it can uphold the throne and the altar, the majesty of the empire, the liberty of the nation, and the rights of the multitude. There is nothing mean, petty, or exclusive, about the real character of Toryism. It necessarily depends upon enlarged sympathies and noble aspirations, because it is essentially national.

[E] *SPEECH FOR HIS BILL TO EXTEND SUFFRAGE TO WORKERS, 1867*[19]

—The fault which had been committed in 1832 in neglecting to give a due share of the representation to the working classes ought to be remedied. . . .

The working classes will now probably have a more extensive sympathy with our political institutions, which, if they are in a healthy state, ought to enlist popular feeling because they should be embodiments of the popular requirements of the country.

For my part, I do not believe that the country is in danger. I think England is safe in the race of men who inhabit her; that she is safe in something much more precious than her accumulated capital—her accumulated experience.

[19] Excerpts from Benjamin Disraeli's speech on the third reading of the Reform Bill of 1867.

[F] CRYSTAL PALACE SPEECH, 1872[20]

This campaign speech created a sensation by rebuking liberal anti-imperialists and inaugurating a new era of vast imperialist expansion.

✓   ✓   ✓

If you look to the history of this country since the advent of liberalism—forty years ago—you will find that there has been no effort so continuous, so subtle, supported by so much energy, and carried on with so much ability and acumen, as the attempts of liberalism to effect the disintegration of the empire of England. . . . Those who advised that policy—and I believe their convictions were sincere—looked upon the colonies of England, looked even upon our connection with India, as a burden upon this country; viewing everything in a financial aspect, and totally passing by those moral and political considerations which make nations great, and by the influence of which alone men are distinguished from animals.

Well, what has been the result of this attempt during the reign of liberalism for the disintegration of the empire? It has entirely failed. But how has it failed? Through the sympathy of the colonies for the mother country. They have decided that the empire shall not be destroyed; and in my opinion no minister in this country will do his duty who neglects any opportunity of reconstructing as much as possible our colonial empire, and of responding to those distant sympathies which may become the source of incalculable strength and happiness to this land. . . .

The issue is not a mean one. It is whether you will be content to be a comfortable England, modeled and molded upon Continental principles and meeting in due course an inevitable fate, or whether you will be a great country, an imperial country, a country where your sons, when they rise, rise to paramount positions, and obtain not merely the esteem of their countrymen, but command the respect of the world.

[20] W. F. Monypenny and G. E. Buckle, *Life of Disraeli,* London, two-volume edition of 1929, II, 534-536.

— Document 12 —

ALEXIS DE TOCQUEVILLE: [A] *DEMOCRACY IN AMERICA*, 1835, 1840[21]

The most balanced of "liberal conservatives" assesses the conflict between traditional frameworks ("forms") and mass democracy; between the individual and conformity.

✓   ✓   ✓

The power of the majority itself is not unlimited. Above it in the moral world are humanity, justice, and reason; and in the political world, vested rights. . . . Until our time it had been supposed that despotism was odious, under whatever form it appeared. But it is a discovery of modern days that there are such things as legitimate tyranny and holy injustice, provided they are exercised in the name of the people. . . . I know of no country in which there is so little independence of mind and real freedom of discussion as in America. In any constitutional state in Europe, every sort of religious and political theory may be freely preached and disseminated; for there is no country in Europe so subdued by any single authority as not to protect the man who raises his voice in the cause of truth from the consequences of his hardihood. If he is unfortunate enough to live under an absolute government, the people are often on his side; if he inhabits a free country, he can, if necessary, find a shelter behind the throne. . . . But in a nation where democratic institutions exist, organized like those of the United States, there is but one authority, one element of strength and success, with nothing beyond it. . . .

Equality awakens in men several propensities extremely

[21] Alexis de Tocqueville, *Democracy In America*, New York, Vintage, 1954, I, 434; II, 343-348. French original: *De la Démocratie en Amérique*, Paris, vol. I, 1835, vol. II, 1840. Reprinted by permission of Alfred A. Knopf, Inc.

dangerous to freedom. . . . Men living in democratic
ages do not readily comprehend the utility of forms. . . .
Forms excite their contempt and often their hatred; as
they commonly aspire to none but easy and present grati-
fications, they rush onwards to the object of their desires,
and the slightest delay exasperates them. This same
temper, carried with them into political life, renders
them hostile to forms, which perpetually retard or arrest
them in some of their projects. Yet this objection which
the men of democracies make to forms is the very thing
which renders forms so useful to freedom; for their chief
merit is to serve as a barrier between the strong and
the weak, the ruler and the people, to retard the one and
give the other time to look about him. Forms become
more necessary in proportion as the government becomes
more active and more powerful, while private persons
are becoming more indolent and more feeble. Thus
democratic nations naturally stand more in need of forms
than other nations, and they naturally respect them
less. . . .

[B] *RECOLLECTIONS,* 1848-1852,[22]

*These three passages (topic headings added) are from
memoirs written during France's revolutionary Second
Republic of 1848-1852. The first passages shows Tocqueville as reluctant prophet of the coming age of mass
revolt; conservative are his admiration for "ancient customs" and his distrust of "universal voting," then a new
panacea. The second passage shows his evolutionary
middle road, conserving a value-framework against socialist and royalist extremes alike; contrast this Burkean
approach with Maistre's royalism. The third passage shows
a Burkean distrust of abstractions.*

[22] Tocqueville, *Recollections,* translated by A. T. de Mattos,
London, 1948; pp. 68, 85, 120, 238, 304. French original:
Souvenirs, Paris, 1893, published posthumously. The second paragraph under the topic "Against Absolutist Systems" comes from his *Democracy In America* but has
been quoted here in order to accompany the closely
related paragraph from *Recollections.*

✓   ✓   ✓
Prophet of Mass-Revolts

The universal voting had shaken the country from top
to bottom without bringing to light a single new man
worthy of coming to the front. . . . A socialistic character to the Revolution of February [*1848*] . . . was not
of a nature to cause such great surprise as it did. Had
it not long been perceived that the people had continually
been improving and raising its condition, that its importance, its education, its desires, its power had been constantly increasing? Its prosperity had also grown greater,
but less rapidly, and was approaching the limit which it
hardly ever passes in old societies, where there are many
men and but few places. How should the poor and
humble and yet powerful classes not have dreamt of issu-
ing from their poverty and inferiority by means of their
power, especially in an epoch when our view into another
world has become dimmer, and the miseries of this world
become more visible and seem more intolerable? They
had been working to this end for the last sixty years. . . .
This inevitable perturbation of its thoughts and its desires, these needs, these instincts of the crowd formed in
a certain sense the fabric upon which the political innovators embroidered so many monstrous and grotesque
figures. Their work may be regarded as ludicrous, but the
material on which they worked is the most serious that it
is possible for philosophers and statesmen to contemplate.

Will Socialism remain buried in the disdain with which
the Socialists of 1848 are so justly covered? . . . I do
not doubt that the laws concerning the constitution of our
modern society will in the long run undergo modification.
. . . The field of possibilities is much more extensive than
men living in their various societies are ready to imagine.
. . . England [*is*] protected against the revolutionary
sickness of nations by the wisdom of her laws and the
strength of her ancient customs. . . .

Against Left and Right Extremes
(*Socialists and Royalists*)

For the first time since I had entered public life, I felt
myself caught in the current of a majority. . . . This
majority would disown the Socialists and the Mon-
tagnards [*Jacobins*] but was sincere in its desire to maintain and organize the Republic. I was with it on those

two leading points: I had no monarchic faith, no affection nor regrets for any prince; I felt called upon to defend no cause save that of liberty and the dignity of mankind. To protect the ancient laws of society against the innovators with the help of the new force which the republican principle might lend to the government; to cause the evident will of the French people to triumph over the passions and desires of the Paris workmen; to conquer demagogism by democracy—that was my only aim. . . . I did not believe then, any more than I do now, that the republican form of government is the best suited to the needs of France. . . . With a people among whom habit, tradition, custom have assured so great a place to the Executive Power, its instability will always be, in periods of excitement, a cause of revolution, and, in peaceful times, a cause of great uneasiness. Moreover I have always considered the Republic an ill-balanced form of government, which always promised more, but gave less, liberty than the Constitutional Monarchy. And yet I sincerely wished to maintain the Republic . . . because I saw nothing ready or fit to set in its place. The old Dynasty was profoundly antipathetic to the majority of the country. . . . One genuine passion remained alive in France: hatred of the Ancien Régime.

Against Absolutist Systems and General Ideas

For my part I detest these absolutist systems which represent all the events of history as depending upon great first causes linked by the chain of fatality, and which, as it were, suppress men from the history of the human race. . . . Antecedent facts, the nature of institutions, the cast of minds and the state of morals are the materials of which are composed those impromptus which astonish and alarm us. . . .

General ideas are no proof of the strength, but rather of the insufficiency of the human intellect; for there are in nature no beings exactly alike, no things precisely identical, no rules indiscriminately and alike applicable to several objects at once. The chief merit of general ideas is that they enable the human mind to pass a rapid judgment on a great many objects at once; but, on the other hand, the notions they convey are never other than incomplete, and they always cause the mind to lose as much in accuracy as it gains in comprehensiveness. . . ,

— Document 13 —

JOHN C. CALHOUN: [A] ON *SLAVERY*, 1838 [23]

Though the doctrines of Burkean conservatism were founded to preserve liberty, they could also—as in these words of Calhoun—be degraded into apologies for slavery.

✓   ✓   ✓

Many in the South once believed that it [*slavery*] was a moral and political evil. That folly and delusion are gone. We see it now in its true light, and regard it as the most safe and stable basis for free institutions in the world.

[B] *A DISQUISITION ON GOVERNMENT*, 1850 [24]

Here is the great Southern conservative's theory of "concurrent majority," as opposed to mob dictatorship of mere numerical majority. The essay appeared posthumously in 1850, was composed several years earlier.

✓   ✓   ✓

There are two different modes in which the sense of the community may be taken; one, simply by the right of suffrage, unaided; the other, by the right through a proper organism. Each collects the sense of the majority. But one regards numbers only, and considers the whole community as a unit, having but one common interest throughout; and collects the sense of the greater number of the whole, as that of the community. The other, on the contrary, regards interests as well as numbers;— considering the community as made up of different and

[23] Quoted in Merle Curti, *The Growth of American Thought*, New York, Harper, 1943, p. 427.
[24] John Calhoun, *Works*, ed. by R. K. Cralle, New York, 1854, I, 28, 30, 35, 38.

conflicting interests, as far as the action of the government is concerned; and takes the sense of each, through its majority or appropriate organ, and the united sense of all, as the sense of the entire community. The former of these I shall call the numerical, or absolute majority; and the latter, the concurrent, or constitutional majority. I call it the constitutional majority, because it is an essential element in every constitutional government,— be its form what it may. So great is the difference, politically speaking, between the two majorities, that they cannot be confounded, without leading to great and fatal errors; and yet the distinction between them has been so entirely overlooked, that when the term *majority* is used in political discussions, it is applied exclusively to designate the numerical,—as if there were no other. . . .

If the numerical majority were really the people; and if, to take its sense truly, were to take the sense of the people truly, a government so constituted would be a true and perfect model of a popular constitutional government; and every departure from it would detract from its excellence. But, as such is not the case,—as the numerical majority, instead of being the people, is only a portion of them,—such a government, instead of being a true and perfect model of the people's government, that is, a people self-governed, is but the government of a part, over a part,—the major over the minor portion. . . .

The concurrent majority is an indispensable element in forming constitutional government; the numerical majority, of itself, must, in all cases, make governments absolute. The necessary consequence of taking the sense of the community by the concurrent majority is to give to each interest or portion of the community a negative on the others. . . . It is this negative power,—the power of preventing or arresting the action of the government,— be it called by what term it may,—veto, interposition, nullification, check, or balance of power,—which, in fact, forms the constitution. . . . The government of the concurrent majority, where the organism is perfect, excludes the possibility of oppression, by giving to each interest, or portion, or order,—where there are established classes,—the means of protecting itself. . . . It is by means of such authorized and effectual resistance, that oppression is prevented, and the necessity of resorting to force superseded, in governments of the concurrent

majority;—and, hence, compromise, instead of force, becomes their conservative principle.

[C] A DISCOURSE ON THE CON-STITUTION AND GOVERNMENT OF THE UNITED STATES, 1850[25]

*Here is the leading statement of states rights and of the
federal rather national character of the Constitution. This
theory became the gospel of Southern conservatives during the Civil War and after, as well as of the States
Rights Party in the 1948 election. Published posthumously,
the "Discourse" was probably composed during 1848-1849.*

↗   ↗   ↗

Nothing more is necessary, in order to show by whom
[*the Constitution*] was ordained and established, than to
ascertain who are meant by,—"We, the people of the
United States"; for, by their authority, it was done. . . .
It was ratified by the several States, through conventions
of delegates, chosen in each State by the people thereof;
and acting, each in the name and by the authority of its
State. . . . "We, the people of the United States of
America," mean the people of the several States of
the Union, acting as free, independent, and sovereign
States. . . . They established it as a compact *between*
them, and not as a constitution *over* them. . . . The
government is federal, and not national. . . . No State
gave the slightest authority to its delegates to form a
national government.

— Document 14 —

THOMAS CARLYLE: PAST AND PRESENT, 1843[26]

[25] *Ibid.*, I, 126, 128, 131, 137, 159.
[26] Thomas Carlyle, *Past and Present*, London, 1843.

Often Carlyle sounded more like what today would be called a fascist nationalist, violent and authoritarian, than a traditional conservative. However, this passage does illustrate perfectly the conservative resentment of the lonely isolation into which a traditional, organic society explodes, under the impact of the cash-nexus of Manchester liberalism.

✓   ✓   ✓

The saddest news is, that we should find our National Existence, as I sometimes hear it said, depend on selling manufactured cotton at a farthing an ell cheaper than any other People. A most narrow stand for a great Nation to base itself on! . . . In brief, all this Mammon-Gospel of Supply-and-Demand, Competition, *Laissez-faire,* and Devil take the hindmost, begins to be one of the shabbiest Gospels ever preached; or altogether the shabbiest. . . . Farthing cheaper per yard! No great Nation can stand on the apex of such a pyramid; screwing itself higher and higher; balancing itself on its great-toe! . . . The inventive genius of great England will not for ever sit patient with mere wheels and pinions, bobbins, straps and billy-rollers whirring in the head of it. The inventive genius of England is not a Beaver's, or a Spinner's or Spider's genius: it is a *Man's* genius, I hope, with a God over him! *Laissez-faire,* Supply-and-Demand—one begins to weary of all that. . . . Trade never so well freed, and Tariffs all settled or abolished, and Supply-and-Demand in full operation—let us all know that we have yet done nothing; that we have merely cleared the ground for doing.

I will venture to believe that in no time, since the beginnings of Society, was the lot of those same dumb millions of toilers so entirely unbearable as it is even in the days now passing over us. . . . That I have been called, by all the Newspapers, a "free man" will avail me little, if my pilgrimage have ended in death and wreck. . . . Liberty requires new definitions. . . . The liberty of not being oppressed by your fellow man is an indispensable yet one of the most insignificant fractional parts of Human Liberty. . . . The notion that a man's liberty consists of giving him the vote at election-hustings, and saying "Behold now I too have my twenty-thousandth part of a Talker in our National Palaver; will not all the gods be good to me?" is one of the pleasantest! . . . The liberty especially which has to purchase itself by social isolation, and each man standing separate from the other, having "no business with him" but a cash-account: this is such a liberty as the earth seldom saw—as the earth will not long put up with, recommend it how you may. . . . Brethren, we know but imperfectly yet, after ages of Constitutional Government, what Liberty and Slavery are.

— Document 15 —

DON JUAN DONOSO CORTÉS: *ESSAY ON CATHOLICISM, AUTHORITY AND ORDER,* 1851 [27]

Out of print in America and still little known here, this essay is gradually coming to be recognized as the greatest single document ever produced by the "reactionary" Maistre wing of conservatism, as opposed to the partly "liberal" Burkean wing. The style alternates between powerful poetic intensity and scintillant but over-cerebral paradoxes. Note, above all, the stress of this Spanish monarchist on evil being innate in man, not in institutions; hence not to be removed by external or democratic reforms.

✓   ✓   ✓

[27] Don Juan Donoso Cortés, Marquis of Valdegamas, *An Essay on Catholicism, Authority and Order,* translated by Mrs. M. V. Goddard, New York and London, new edition of 1925, pp. 172-176, 205-208, 188-192, 195-197, 126, 140-141, 348-351. Original Spanish title: *Ensayo sobre el Catolicismo, el Liberalismo y el Socialismo.* The italicized topic headings, here inserted for reader convenience, were not in the original.

Against Relativist Liberalism

The liberal school . . . is placed between two seas, whose constantly advancing waves will finally overwhelm it, between socialism and Catholicism. . . . It cannot admit the constituent sovereignty of the people without becoming democratic, socialistic, and atheistic, nor admit the actual sovereignty of God without becoming monarchical and Catholic. . . . This school is only dominant when society is threatened with dissolution, and the moment of its authority is that transitory and fugitive one in which the world stands doubting between Barabbas and Jesus and hesitates between a dogmatical affirmation and a supreme negation. At such a time, society willingly allows itself to be governed by a school which never *affirms* nor *denies,* but is always making distinctions. . . . Such periods of agonizing doubt can never last any great length of time. . . . Man was born to act . . . and will resolutely declare either for Barabbas or Jesus, and overturn all that the sophists have attempted to establish.

The socialist schools . . . possess great advantages over the liberal school, precisely because they approach directly all great problems and questions, and always give a peremptory and decisive solution. The strength of socialism consists in its being a system of theology, and it is destructive only because it is a satanic theology. The socialist schools, as they are theological, will prevail over the liberal, because the latter is antitheological and skeptical. But they themselves, on account of their satanic element, will be vanquished by the Catholic school, which is at the same time theological and divine. The instincts of socialism would seem to agree with our affirmations, since it hates Catholicism, while it [*merely*] despises liberalism.

Against Socialism and Atheism

All the socialist schools are, in a philosophical point of view, rationalistic; under a political aspect, atheistical. They resemble the liberal school in their elements of rationalism, and differ from this school in so far as they are atheistical and republican. . . . To dogmatically affirm the existence of God, after having dogmatically despoiled Him of all His attributes, is an inconsistency reserved for the liberal school. . . .

The socialists appear bold in their negations only when we compare them with the liberalists, who see in each affirmation a difficulty and in each negation a danger. But the timidity of the socialists strikes us at once if we compare them with the Catholic school. For then we perceive with what confidence the latter affirms, and with what timidity the former deny. What! you call yourselves the apostles of a new gospel, and speak to us about evil and sin, redemption and grace, things which are all found in the old gospel! You claim to be the depositaries of a new political, social, and religious science, and yet speak to us of liberty, equality, and fraternity, things all as old as Catholicism, which is as old as the world! He who has declared that He would exalt the lowly and would humble the proud, has fulfilled His word in your case; for He has condemned you to be only the blind expounders of His immortal Gospel by the very fact of your aspiring, with a wild and foolish ambition, to promulgate a new law from a new Sinai but not from a new Calvary!

Conservatism Defined as Emphasis on Evil in Man, not in Institutions

The liberal school holds it as certain that there is no evil except that which results from the political institutions which we have inherited from past ages, and that the supreme good consists in the overthrow of these institutions. The greater number of socialists consider it as established that there is no other evil than that which exists in society, and that the great remedy is to be found in the complete subversion of social institutions. All agree that evil is transmitted to us from past ages. The liberals affirm that good may be realized even in the present day, while the socialists assert that this golden era cannot commence except in times yet to come.

Thus, both the one and the other, placing the realization of the supreme good in the entire destruction of the present order—the political order, according to the liberal school, and the social order, according to the socialist schools—they agree with regard to the real and intrinsic goodness of man, who, they contend, must necessarily be the intelligent and free agent in effecting this subversion. This conclusion has been explicitly an-

nounced by the socialist schools, and it is implicitly contained in the theory maintained by the liberals. The conclusion is so far maintained in this theory that, if you
deny the conclusion, the theory itself must fall to the
ground. In fact, the theory, according to which evil exists
in man, and proceeds from man, contradicts that other
theory, which supposes evil to exist in political and social
institutions, and to proceed from them. If we adopt the
first hypothesis, there would exist a logical necessity to
commence by eradicating evil from the heart of man,
in order to extirpate it from society and the state. If we
adopt the second supposition, the logical consequence
would be the necessity of commencing by eradicating
evil directly from society or the state, where it has its
center and origin.

From this we see that the Catholic and rationalist
theories are not only utterly incompatible, but likewise
antagonistic. All subversion, whether it be in the political
or social order, is condemned by the Catholic theory as
foolish and useless. The rationalist theories condemn all
moral reform in man as stupid and of no avail. Thus,
both the socialist and the liberal theories are consistent
in their condemnation; because, if evil exists neither in
the state nor in society, why and wherefore require the
overthrow of society and of the state? And, on the contrary, if evil neither exists in individuals nor proceeds
from them, why and for what cause desire the interior
reformation of man? . . .

If we adopt the theory of the innate and absolute
goodness of man, then he is the universal reformer,
and in no need of being himself reformed. This view
transforms man into God, and he ceases to have a human
nature and becomes divine. Being in himself absolute
goodness, the effect produced by the revolutions he creates must be absolute good; and as the chief good, and
cause of all good, man must therefore be most excellent,
most wise, and most powerful. Adoration is so imperative
a necessity for man that we find the socialists, who are
atheists, and as such refusing to adore God, making
gods of men, and in this way inventing a new form of
adoration. . . .

The Catholics affirm that evil comes from man, and
redemption from God; the socialists affirm that evil

comes from society, and redemption from man. The two affirmations of Catholicism are sensible and natural, namely, that man is man, and performs human works, and that God is God, and performs divine acts. The two affirmations of socialism assert that man understands and executes the designs of God, and that society performs the works proper to man. What, then, does human reason gain when it rejects Catholicism for socialism? Does it not refuse to receive that which is evident and mysterious, in order to accept that which is at once mysterious and absurd?

Conservative Faith in Order and Retribution

If sin consists in disobedience and rebellion, and if these are nothing but disorder, and disorder nothing but evil, then it follows that evil, disorder, rebellion, disobedience, and sin are absolutely identical—just as good, order, submission, and obedience are things presenting a perfect resemblance. . . . The rebellion of the angel was the first disorder, the first evil, and the first sin. . . .

From the perpetual necessity of order results the perpetual necessity of the existence of the physical and moral laws which constitute it. . . . The world has in vain rejected these laws. In seeking by their negation to throw off this yoke, they have only succeeded in making its weight more heavy, because a departure from these laws always produces catastrophes. . . . God has permitted to human opinion a free and wide range: . . . dominion over the sea and land, and the power to rebel against his Creator; to revolt against heaven; to form treaties and covenants with infernal spirits; to deafen the world with the din of battle; to excite discord and contention in societies, and terrify them by the fearful shock of revolutions; . . . to declare an independence of all authority. . . . All this and much more was given to man; yet the stars pursue their appointed courses and forever continue in harmonious progression. . . . Man has been allowed to crush society, agitated by the discord which he has fomented . . . but it has not been permitted him to suspend for one single day, hour, or minute, the infallible accomplishment of the fundamental laws which regulate the moral and physical world. . . . The world has never seen, and will never see, the man who has

departed through sin from the laws of order, and who
has been able to escape a conformity with those laws by
means of punishment, that messenger of God which all
men must receive.

— Document 16 —

JAKOB BURCKHARDT: *PREDICTIONS OF TOTALITARIANISM,* 1864-1893 [98]

*Some of these uncanny warnings of the great Swiss
conservative are here translated into English for the first
time. They re-interpreted democratic mass equality as
breeding the tyrannies later known as fascism and communism.*

✓   ✓   ✓

Everywhere the forces from below are on the march
upward, even when they have not yet triumphed at the
polls. . . . Security is at an end ever since politics has
been based on mass ferment. . . . It would be a real
gain if we could get rid of that infamous, unjust piece
of terminology: "the working classes." . . . The people
are being trained for mass meetings. It will end up with
their howling whenever there are not at least a hundred
of them in one place. . . . I would not be criticizing the
dreadful increase in mass education if it were only a
matter of costing money. But it will create endless generations of malcontents in the new Europe. . . .

The big damage was done in the previous [*eighteenth*]

[98] First two paragraphs are translated by P. Viereck from
Jakob Burckhardt, *Briefe an seinen Freund Friedrich von
Preen: 1864-1893,* Stuttgart, 1922, pp. 35-36, 51, 73, 104,
117, 130, 158, 178, 196, 262. Paragraphs three and four:
Briefe an einen Architekten: 1870-1889, Munich, 1913,
pp. 176, 221. Last paragraph: *Historische Fragmente aus
dem Nachlass* included in *Gesamtausgabe,* Stuttgart, 1929,
p. 246.

century, especially by Rousseau with his preaching of the goodness of human nature. . . . As any child can see, this resulted in the complete dissolution of the concept of [*legitimate*] authority in the heads of mortals, whereupon they periodically had to be subjected to naked [*illegitimate*] force instead. The only imaginable solution would be if at last everybody, big and small, would get that crazy optimism [*about progress*] out of his head. . . . The world approaches two alternatives, either full democracy or an absolute lawless despotism. The latter will no longer be run by dynasties, for these are too soft-hearted, but by a military command disguised as republicanism. . . . A real power is building up which will make damned short work of suffrage, popular sovereignty, material welfare, industry, etc. . . . I have a premonition which sounds like utter folly, and yet it will not leave me: the military state will become one single vast factory. Those hordes of men in the great industrial centers cannot be left indefinitely to their greed and want. What must logically come is a definite and supervised stint of misery, with promotions and uniforms, daily begun and ended to the sound of drums. . . . In the delightful twentieth century, authoritarianism will raise its head again, and a terrifying head it will be.

. . . The fall of Greece began with the rise of democracy there. For a few decades, Greece managed to live on the reserve capital of its great strength, thereby giving the illusion that this strength was the product of democracy. After that, Greece was doomed; and the later terrifying development of Greek life was survived only by art. . . .

In order to get re-elected, the leaders of the populace must win the excitement-craving masses. The masses demand constant action; otherwise they will not believe that "progress" is taking place. It is impossible to escape from this vicious circle of universal suffrage. So long as the masses can bring pressure on their leaders, one value after another must be sacrificed: position, property, religion, distinguished tradition, higher learning. . . . This force can come only from the worst elements, and its consequences will make your hair stand on end.

My picture of the terrible simplifiers (*terribles simplificateurs*) is no pleasant one. . . . Naked force in command and the silencing of opposition. . . .

— Document 17 —

FEODOR DOSTOYEVSKY: *NOTES FROM UNDERGROUND*, 1864[29]

The "cultural conservative" was defined in Chapter 1 as the tormented anti-massman who questions democratic material progress. Without accepting Dostoyevsky's intolerant tsarist political conservatism, one can forever learn from his psychological perceptions as "cultural conservatism" at its profoundest.

✓   ✓   ✓

You gentlemen have taken your whole register of human advantages from the averages of statistical figures and politico-economical formulas. . . . Shower upon man every earthly blessing, drown him in a sea of happiness, so that nothing but bubbles of bliss can be seen on the surface; give him economic prosperity such that he should have nothing else to do but sleep, eat cakes, and busy himself with the continuation of his species; and even then, out of sheer ingratitude, sheer spite, man would play you some nasty trick. He would even risk his cakes and would deliberately desire the most fatal rubbish, the most uneconomical absurdity, simply to introduce into all this positive good sense his final fantastic element . . . simply to prove to himself—as though that were necessary—that men are still men and not the keys of a piano. . . . The whole work of man really seems to consist in nothing but proving to himself every minute that he is a man and not a piano key.

[29] Feodor Dostoyevsky (Dostoevsky), *Short Novels of Dostoevsky,* translated by Constance Garnett, New York, 1945, pp. 142, 149.

JOHN HENRY NEWMAN: *APOLOGIA PRO VITA SUA*, 1864 [30]

Characteristically conservative in Cardinal Newman's sensitively written autobiography is the stress on Original Sin.

I had fierce thoughts against the Liberals. It was the success of the Liberal cause which fretted me inwardly. I became fierce against its instruments and its manifestations. A French vessel was at Algiers; I would not even look at the tricolour. . . .

I argue about the world;—*if* there be a God, *since* there is a God, the human race is implicated in some terrible aboriginal calamity. It is out of joint with the purposes of its Creator. This is a fact, a fact as true as the fact of its existence; and thus the doctrine of what is theologically called *original sin* becomes to me almost as certain as that the world exists, and as the existence of God. . . . Religious men, external to the Catholic Church, have attempted various expedients to arrest fierce wilful human nature. . . . But where was the concrete representative of things invisible, which would have the force and the toughness necessary to be a breakwater against the deluge?

[B] APPENDIX ON *LIBERALISM*, 1865 [31]

[30] John Henry Newman, *Apologia Pro Vita Sua,* New York & London, 1892 edition, pp. 242-244.
[31] *Op. cit.,* pp. 285-297.

Newman added this appendix to the 1865 edition of his Apologia of 1864 in order to rebut liberal objections and to list eighteen liberal tenets he condemned; cf. those listed by Pius IX in 1864 (Document 19).

✓   ✓   ✓

Liberty of thought is in itself a good; but it gives an opening to false liberty. Now by Liberalism I mean false liberty of thought, or the exercise of thought upon matters in which, from the constitution of the human mind, thought cannot be brought to any successful issue, and therefore is out of place. Among such matters are first principles of whatever kind. . . . Liberalism, then, is the mistake of subjecting to human judgment those revealed doctrines which are in their nature beyond and independent of it. . . . I conclude this notice of Liberalism in Oxford . . . with some propositions . . . I earnestly denounced and abjured.

1. No religious tenet is important, unless reason shows it to be so.

Therefore, e.g. the doctrine of the Athanasian Creed is not to be insisted on, unless it tends to convert the soul; and the doctrine of the Atonement is to be insisted on, if it does convert the soul.

2. No one can believe what he does not understand.

Therefore, e.g. there are no mysteries in true religion.

3. No theological doctrine is any thing more than an opinion which happens to be held by bodies of men.

Therefore, e.g. no creed, as such, is necessary for salvation.

4. It is dishonest in a man to make an act of faith in what he has not had brought home to him by actual proof.

Therefore, e.g. the mass of men ought not absolutely to believe in the divine authority of the Bible.

5. It is immoral in a man to believe more than he can spontaneously receive as being congenial to his moral and mental nature.

Therefore, e.g. a given individual is not bound to believe in eternal punishment.

6. No revealed doctrines or precepts may reasonably stand in the way of scientific conclusions.

Therefore, e.g. Political Economy may reverse our Lord's declarations about poverty and riches, or a sys-

NEWMAN: APPENDIX ON LIBERALISM 163

*tem of Ethics may teach that the highest condition of
body is ordinarily essential to the highest state of mind.*

7. Christianity is necessarily modified by the growth
of civilization, and the exigencies of times.

*Therefore, e.g. the Catholic priesthood, though neces-
sary in the Middle Ages, may be superseded now.*

8. There is a system of religion more simply true than
Christianity as it has ever been received.

*Therefore, e.g. we may advance that Christianity is the
"corn of wheat" which has been dead for 1800 years, but
at length will bear fruit; and that Mahometanism is the
manly religion, and existing Christianity the womanish.*

9. There is a right of Private Judgment: that is, there
is no existing authority on earth competent to interfere
with the liberty of individuals in reasoning and judging
for themselves about the Bible and its contents, as they
severally please.

*Therefore, e.g. religious establishments requiring sub-
scription are Anti-christian.*

10. There are rights of conscience such, that every
one may lawfully advance a claim to profess and teach
what is false and wrong in matters, religious, social, and
moral, provided that to his private conscience it seems
absolutely true and right.

*Therefore, e.g. individuals have a right to preach and
practice fornication and polygamy.*

11. There is no such thing as a national or state conscience.

*Therefore, e.g. no judgments can fall upon a sinful
or infidel nation.*

12. The Civil Power has no positive duty, in a normal state of things, to maintain religious truth.

*Therefore, e.g. blasphemy and sabbath-breaking are not
rightly punishable by law.*

13. Utility and expedience are the measure of political
duty.

*Therefore, e.g. no punishment may be enacted, on the
ground that God commands it: e.g. on the text, "Whoso
sheddeth man's blood, by man shall his blood be shed."*

14. The Civil Power may dispose of Church property
without sacrilege.

*Therefore, e.g. Henry VIII committed no sin in his
spoliations.*

15. The Civil Power has the right of ecclesiastical

jurisdiction and administration.

Therefore, e.g. Parliament may impose articles of faith on the Church or suppress Dioceses.

16. It is lawful to rise in arms against legitimate princes.

Therefore, e.g. the Puritans in the 17th century, and the French in the 18th, were justifiable in their Rebellion and Revolution respectively.

17. The people are the legitimate source of power.

Therefore, e.g. Universal Suffrage is among the natural rights of man.

18. Virtue is the child of knowledge, and vice of ignorance.

Therefore, e.g. education, periodical literature, railroad travelling, ventilation, drainage, and the arts of life, when fully carried out, serve to make a population moral and happy.

— Document 19 —

PIUS IX: *SYLLABUS OF ERRORS,* 1864 [32]

This rebuke to scientific liberalism by Pope Pius IX (1846-1878) is the most uncompromisingly right-wing document produced by modern Catholicism. Since the "syllabus" is worded negatively, each clause should be prefaced by the words "It is not true that. . . ." The reader may contrast this encyclical with the more conciliatory one of Pope Leo XIII, cited on p. 55.

✓   ✓   ✓

Presenting the principal errors of our time, which are stigmatized in the consistorial allocutions, encyclicals, and other apostolic letters of our most holy lord, Pope Pius the Ninth.

Section 1: Pantheism, Naturalism, and Rationalism Absolute

[32] Pope Pius IX, *The Papal Encyclical and Syllabus, Literally Translated from the Authorized Latin Text,* London, 1875, pp. 13-15, 20.

1. There exists no Divine Being, perfect in His wisdom and goodness, who is distinct from the universe, and God is of the same nature as things, and consequently subject to change; in effect, God is produced in man and in the world, and all beings are God, and have the same substance as God. God is thus one and the same thing with the world; consequently the mind is the same thing with matter, necessity with liberty, the true with the false, the good with the evil, and the just with the unjust.—2. All action of God upon man and upon the world is to be denied.—3. Human reason, without any regard to God, is the sole arbiter of truth and falsehood, of good and evil; it is a law to itself, and by its natural force it suffices to secure the welfare of men and nations.—4. All the truths of religion are derived from the inborn strength of human reason; hence it follows that reason is the sovereign rule by which men can and ought to acquire knowledge of all truth of every kind. . . .

Section 2: Moderate Rationalism

8. As human reason is on an equality with religion itself, so the theological sciences ought to be treated in the same manner as the philosophical sciences. . . . 11. The Church ought not only never to animadvert upon philosophy, but it ought even to tolerate its errors, leaving to philosophy the care of correcting itself.—12. The decrees of the Apostolic See and of the Roman Congregation prevent the free progress of science.

Section 7: Errors Concerning Natural and Christian Morality

56. Moral laws do not need the divine sanction, and there is no necessity that human laws should be conformable to the law of nature, or receive from God the power of binding.—57. Knowledge of philosophical things and morals, as well as civil laws, may and ought to be independent of divine and ecclesiastical authority. —58. No other forces should be recognized than those which reside in matter, and all moral teaching and moral excellence should consist in accumulating and augmenting riches in every possible way, and in satisfying the passions.—59. Right consists in material action; all the duties of men are words devoid of sense and all human actions have the force of right.—60. Authority is nothing else

than the result of numbers and material forces.—76.
The abolition of the temporal power, of which the Holy
See is possessed, would contribute in the greatest degree
to the liberty and prosperity of the Church.—77. In
the present day, it is no longer expedient that the Catholic religion shall be held as the only religion of the
State, to the exclusion of all other modes of worship.—
78. Whence it has been wisely provided by law, in some
countries called Catholic, that persons coming to reside
therein shall enjoy the public exercise of their own worship.—80. The Roman Pontiff can and ought to reconcile
himself to, and agree with progress, liberalism and civilization as lately introduced.

— Document 20 —

LOUIS VEUILLOT: *THE LIBERAL ILLUSION*, 1866 [33]

*Supported by Cortés and by Pius IX, the French editor
Veuillot fought unrelentingly against those of his fellow
Catholics who were willing to come to terms with modern
liberal democracy.*

✓   ✓   ✓

In the normal order, Christian society is maintained
and extended by means of two powers. . . . The first
sword, the one that cleaves nothing but darkness, remains
in the patient and infallibly enlightened power of the
Pontiff. The other, the material sword, is in the hand
of the representative of society, and in order that it may
make no mistake, it is in duty bound to obey the com-
mandment of the Pontiff. . . . Liberal Catholicism has
no value whatever either as a doctrine or as a means of
defending religion. . . . It behooves us to lock arms
around the Sovereign Pontiff, . . . to affirm with him

[33] Louis Veuillot, *The Liberal Illusion,* tr. by George Barry
    O'Toole, Washington, 1939, pp. 37-38, 38-39, 47-48, 62-
    64, 76-77.

the truths that alone can save our souls and the world.
. . . The doctrines known as liberal have riven us apart.

— Document 21 —

HENRY SUMNER MAINE:
POPULAR GOVERNMENT, 1885 [34]

Distinguishing between liberty and democratic equality, this British political scientist argued that the American and British constitutions give liberty not because they are democratic but because they restrict democracy.

✓   ✓   ✓

Two of the historical watchwords of democracy exclude one another. . . . Where there is political liberty, there can be no equality. . . . The French threw away universal suffrage after the Reign of Terror; it was twice revived in France that the Napoleonic tyranny might be founded on it. . . . This observation [*by the historian Taine*], that "a human society, and particularly a modern society is a vast and complicated thing," is in fact the very proposition which Burke enforced. . . . The British Constitution . . . is unique and remarkable. . . . The imitations have not been generally happy. . . . The only evidence worth mentioning for the duration of popular government is to be found in the success of the British Constitution during two centuries under special conditions, and in the success of the American Constitution during one century under conditions still more peculiar and more unlikely to recur. . . .

American experience has, I think, shown that, [*solely*] by wise Constitutional provisions thoroughly thought out beforehand, Democracy may be made tolerable. The public powers are carefully defined: the mode in which they are to be exercised is fixed; and the amplest securities are taken that none of the more important Constitutional arrangements shall be altered without every guarantee of caution. . . .

[34] Sir Henry Sumner Maine, *Popular Government*, New York, 1886, pp. 29-55. Original British edition, 1885.

FRIEDRICH NIETZSCHE: [A] *BEYOND GOOD AND EVIL,* 1886[35]

The loneliest and most independent mind of the century foresaw not liberty but tyranny as the fruit of democratic equality. Cf. Document 16 by his friend Burckhardt.

     ✓   ✓   ✓

. . . "Equality of rights" could all too easily be converted into an equality in violating rights—by that I mean, into a common war on all that is rare, strange, or privileged, on the higher man, the higher soul, the higher duty, the higher responsibility, and on the wealth of creative power and mastery—today the concept of "greatness" entails being noble, wanting to be by oneself, being capable of being different, standing alone. . . .

It is the age of the masses: they lie on their belly before everything that is massive. And so also in politics. A statesman who rears up for them a new Tower of Babel, some monstrosity of empire and power, they call "great"—what does it matter that we more prudent and conservative ones do not meanwhile give up the old belief that it is only the great thought that gives greatness to an action? . . .

The democratic movement in Europe . . . will probably arrive at results on which its naïve propagators and panegyrists, the apostles of "modern ideas," would least care to reckon. The same new conditions under which on an average a leveling and mediocritising of man will take place—a clever gregarious man—are in the highest

---

[35] Friedrich Nietzsche, *Jenseits von Gut und Boese,* 1886. For a clear rendering, no single translation sufficed. The first paragraph used is from *The Portable Nietzsche,* ed. by W. Kaufmann, New York, Viking, 1954; p. 446. Second paragraph: *Beyond Good and Evil,* Modern Library edition, New York, Random, n.d.; p. 172. Third paragraph: *Works of Nietzsche,* ed. by Orson Falk, New York, Tudor, 1931; I, 173-174.

degree suitable to give rise to exceptional men of the most dangerous and attractive qualities. For, while the capacity for adaptation, which is every day trying changing conditions, and begins a new work with every generation, almost with every decade, makes the powerfulness of the type impossible; while the collective impression of such future Europeans will probably be that of numerous, talkative, weak-willed, and very handy workmen who *require* a master, a commander, as they require their daily bread; while, therefore, the democratising of Europe will tend to the production of a type prepared for *slavery* in the most subtle sense of the term; the strong man will necessarily in individual and exceptional cases, become stronger and richer than he has perhaps ever been before—owing to the unprejudicedness of his schooling, owing to the immense variety of practice, art, and disguise. . . . The democratising of Europe is at the same time an involuntary arrangement for the rearing of tyrants. . . .

[B] *TWILIGHT OF THE GODLINGS,* 1889 [36]

Cultural conservatism sees politics of whatever kind as shallow and as a drain on culture.

✓   ✓   ✓

Heavy is the price of coming to power: power makes its possessor stupid. . . . "Deutschland, Deutschland ueber alles" [*national anthem*], I fear that has ended German philosophy. . . . You cannot live beyond your means, whether as an individual or as a nation. Both

---

[36] Translated by P. Viereck from Nietzsche, *Die Goetzen-Daemmerung,* 1889; *Gesammelte Werke,* Munich, 1920-1929, vol. 17, VIII, 1-4. "Idols" for "Goetzen" in other English translations, while literally more correct, sacrifices the author's obvious purpose of a play on words with "Goetter." Likewise in most English translations of his texts themselves, a literal rendering misses the nuances; these depend not on the denotations alone but on the kinaesthetic connotations of his nervous rhythms, his quick and never accidental changes of pace.

possess certain limited energies of understanding, seriousness, will, and self-transcendence; if you squander these energies on the side of power, power politics, economics, world trade, parliaments, and armies, then you cannot spend them on the cultural side. Culture and the state—let there be no wishful thinking about this—are enemies. The one flourishes at the expense of the other. All great epochs of culture have been epochs of political decline. What is culturally great has always been unpolitical, even antipolitical.

— Document 23 —

KONSTANTIN PETROVICH POBIEDONOSTSEV: *REFLECTIONS OF A RUSSIAN STATESMAN,* 1898 [37]

Here is the most "reactionary" single document in our entire selection. This official spokesman for tsarist autocracy was chief adviser of Alexander III and, until 1905, of Nicholas II.

✔   ✔   ✔

The passionate apostles of freedom mistake in assuming freedom in equality. Bitter experience has proven a hundred times that freedom does not depend from equality, and that equality is in no wise freedom. . . .

What is this freedom by which so many minds are agitated, which inspires so many insensate actions, so many wild speeches, which leads the people so often to misfortune? In the democratic sense of the word, freedom is the right of political power, or, to express it otherwise, the right to participate in the government of the State. This universal aspiration for a share in government has

[37] Pobyedonostseff (Pobiedonostsev), Konstantin Petrovich, *Reflections of a Russian Statesman,* trans. by R. C. Long, London, Grant Richards, 1898, *passim.* The original Russian edition was entitled *Moscow Conversations.*

no constant limitations, and seeks no definite issue, but incessantly extends. . . . Forever extending its base, the new Democracy now aspires to universal suffrage—a fatal error, and one of the most remarkable in the history of mankind. By this means, the political power so passionately demanded by Democracy would be shattered into a number of infinitesimal bits, of which each citizen acquires a single one. Each vote, representing an inconsiderable fragment of power, by itself signifies nothing. . . . He who controls a number of these fragmentary forces is master of all power. . . . In a Democracy, the real rulers are the dexterous manipulators of votes, with their placemen, the mechanics who so skilfully operate the hidden springs which move the puppets in the arena of democratic elections. Men of this kind are ever ready with loud speeches lauding equality; in reality, they rule the people as any despot or military dictator might rule it.

The extension of the right to participate in elections is regarded as progress and as the conquest of freedom by democratic theorists, who hold that the more numerous the participants in political rights, the greater is the probability that all will employ this right in the interests of the public welfare, and for the increase of the freedom of the people. Experience proves a very different thing. The history of mankind bears witness that the most necessary and fruitful reforms—the most durable measures—emanated from the supreme will of one statesman, or from a minority enlightened by lofty ideas and deep knowledge, and that, on the contrary, the extension of the representative principle is accompanied by an abasement of political ideas and the vulgarisation of opinions in the mass of the electors. It shows also that this extension—in great States—was inspired by secret aims to the centralization of power, or led directly to dictatorship. In France, universal suffrage was suppressed with the end of the Terror, and was re-established twice merely to affirm the autocracy of the two Napoleons. In Germany, the establishment of universal suffrage served merely to strengthen the high authority of a famous statesman who had acquired popularity by the success of his policy. What its ultimate consequences will be, Heaven only knows!

Among the falsest of political principles is the principle of the sovereignty of the people, the principle that all power issues from the people, and is based upon the national will—a principle which has unhappily become more firmly established since the time of the French Revolution. Thence proceeds the theory of Parliamentarism, which, up to the present day, has deluded much of the so-called "intelligence," and unhappily infatuated certain foolish Russians. . . . In what does the theory of Parliamentarism consist? It is supposed that the people in its assemblies makes its own laws, and elects responsible officers to execute its will. . . . [But] on the day of polling few give their votes intelligently; these are the individuals, influential electors whom it has been worth while to convince in private. The mass of electors, after the practice of the herd, votes for one of the candidates nominated by the committees. Not one exactly knows the man, or considers his character, his capacity, his convictions; all vote merely because they have heard his name so often. It would be vain to struggle against this herd. . . .

In theory, the election favors the intelligent and capable; in reality, it favors the pushing and impudent. It might be thought that education, experience, conscientiousness in work, and wisdom in affairs, would be essential requirements in the candidate; in reality, whether these qualities exist or not, they are in no way needed in the struggle of the election, where the essential qualities are audacity, a combination of impudence and oratory, and even some vulgarity, which invariably acts on the masses; modesty, in union with delicacy of feeling and thought, is worth nothing. . . .

The importance of the Press is immense, and may be regarded as the most characteristic fact of our time. . . . No government, no law, no custom can withstand its destructive activity. . . . Whence is derived their right and authority to rule in the name of the community, to demolish existing institutions, and to proclaim new ideals of ethics and legislation? But no one attempts to answer this question; all talk loudly of the liberty of the Press as the first and essential element of social well-being. Even in Russia, so libelled by the lying Press of Europe, such words are heard. . . . How often have superficial and unscrupulous journalists paved the way for revolution, fomented irritation into enmity, and brought about desolating wars! For conduct such as this a monarch would lose his throne, a minister would be disgraced, impeached, and punished; but the journalist stands dry above the waters he has disturbed, from the ruin he has caused he rises triumphant, and briskly continues his destructive work.

. . . The natural instinct of man seeks for power in unbroken activity, to which the mass, with its varied needs, aspirations, and passions may submit; through which it may acquire the impulse of activity, and the principles of order; in which it may find amid all the subversions of wilfulness a standard of truth. . . . Power is great and terrible, because it is a sacred thing. . . . Power exists not for itself alone, but for the love of God; it is a service to which men are dedicated. Thence comes the limitless, terrible strength of power, and its limitless and terrible burden. . . . From this also springs the creative force of power, the strength to attract just and rational men. . . . To power belongs the first and last word—it is the alpha and omega of human activity. . . .

Thus the work of power is a work of uninterrupted usefulness, and in reality a work of renunciation. How strange these words must seem beside the current conception of power! . . . Yet the immutable, only true ideal of power is embodied in the words of Christ: "Whosoever of you will be the chiefest shall be servant of all." . . . The first necessity of power is faith in itself and in its mission. Happy is power when this faith is combined with a recognition of duty and of moral responsibility!

— Document 24 —

WINSTON S. CHURCHILL: EXCERPTS FROM GREAT SPEECHES, 1903-1946 [38]

[38] The speeches were given in House of Commons unless otherwise stated. The date has been inserted before each excerpt. Sources: the dates in question of the official British *Parliamentary Debates, House of Commons* (Hansard, London, 1903-1940), the *Times* of London, and (in the case of the speech of 1946) *The New York Times.*

*Note Winston Churchill's distinction between aristoc-
racy and plutocracy in 1903, his prophetic warnings
against Communist aggression in 1941 and 1946, and
his Burkean appeals to tradition in rallying a beleaguered
England against the Nazis in 1940. Many of the phrases
here quoted—"blood, tears, and sweat," "their finest
hour," and "iron curtain"—are already immortal.*

✓   ✓   ✓

[*May 28, 1903.*] The new fiscal policy [*of high tariffs*]
means a change, not only in the historic English parties
but in the conditions of our public life. The old Conservative Party with its religious convictions and constitutional principles will disappear and a new party will
arise . . . like perhaps the Republican Party in the
United States of America . . . rigid, materialist and
secular, whose opinions will turn on tariffs and who
will cause the lobbies to be crowded with the touts of
protected industries . . . Not for the last hundred years
has a more surprising departure been suggested.

[*January 3, 1921 at Sunderland.*] Was there ever a more
awful spectacle in the whole history of the world than is
unfolded by the agony of Russia? . . . The theories of
Lenin and Trotsky have fatally, and it may be finally,
ruptured the means of intercourse between man and man,
between workman and peasant. . . . They have driven
man from the civilization of the twentieth century into
a condition of barbarism worse than the Stone Age. . . .
And this is progress, this is liberty, this is Utopia! This
is what my friend in the gallery would call an interesting
experiment in Social Regeneration. What a monstrous
absurdity and perversion of the truth it is, to represent
the Communist theory as a form of progress, when, at
every step and at every stage, it is simply marching back
into the Dark Ages.

[*May 13, 1940.*] I would say to the House, as I said
to those who have joined this Government: "I have nothing to offer but blood, toil, tears and sweat." We have
before us an ordeal of the most grievous kind. . . . You
ask, what is our aim? I can answer in one word: It is
victory, victory at all costs, victory in spite of all terror,
victory, however long and hard the road may be; for
without victory there is no survival. Let that be realized;

no survival for the British Empire; no survival for all that the British Empire has stood for, no survival for the urge and impulse of the ages, that mankind will move forward towards its goal. But I take up my task with buoyancy and hope. I feel sure that our cause will not be suffered to fail among men. At this time I feel entitled to claim the aid of all, and I say, "Come, then, let us go forward together with our united strength."

[*June 4, 1940 on epic of Dunkirk.*] We are told that Herr Hitler has a plan for invading the British Isles. That has often been thought of before. When Napoleon lay at Boulogne for over a year with his flat-bottomed boats and grand army, he was told by someone, "There are bitter weeds in England." . . . We cannot flag or fail. We shall go on to the end. We shall fight in France, we shall fight on the seas and oceans; we shall fight with growing confidence and growing strength in the air. We shall defend our island whatever the cost may be. We shall fight on the beaches, we shall fight on the landing grounds, in the fields, in the streets, and in the hills. We shall never surrender, and even if—which I do not for a moment believe—this island or a large part of it were subjugated and starving, then our Empire beyond the seas, armed and guarded by the British Fleet, will carry on the struggle until, in God's good time, the New World with all its power and might sets forth to the liberation and rescue of the Old.

[*June 18, 1940 on Battle of Britain.*] I expect that the battle of Britain is about to begin. Upon this battle depends the survival of Christian civilization. Upon it depends our own British life and the long continuity of our institutions and our Empire. The whole fury and might of the enemy must very soon be turned on us. Hitler knows that he will have to break us in this island or lose the war. If we can stand up to him, all Europe may be free and the life of the world may move forward into broad, sunlit uplands; but if we fail, then the whole world, including the United States, and all that we have known and cared for, will sink into the abyss of a new dark age made more sinister, and perhaps more prolonged, by the lights of a perverted science. Let us, therefore, brace ourselves to our duty and so bear ourselves that, if the British Commonwealth and Empire lasts for a thousand years, men will still say, "This was their finest hour."

[*March 5, 1946, introduced by President Harry Truman at Fulton, Missouri.*] It would be criminal madness to cast it [*the American atom bomb*] adrift in this agitated and un-united world. No one in any country has slept less well in their beds because this knowledge and the method and the raw materials to apply it, are at present largely retained in American hands. I do not believe we should all have slept so soundly had the positions been reversed, and if some Communist or neo-Fascist State monopolized for the time being these dread agencies. The fear of them alone might easily have been used to enforce totalitarian systems upon the free democratic world, with consequences appalling to human imagination. God has willed that this shall not be, and we have at least a breathing space to set our house in order before this peril has to be encountered. . . . Beware, I say, time may be short. From Stettin in the Baltic to Trieste in the Adriatic, an iron curtain has descended across the Continent. Behind that line lie all the capitals of the ancient states of Central and Eastern Europe. . . . This is certainly not the Liberated Europe we fought to build up. . . . The Communist parties of fifth columns constitute a growing challenge and peril to Christian civilization. These are sombre facts for anyone to have to recite on the morrow of a victory gained by so much splendid comradeship in arms and in the cause of freedom and democracy; but we should be most unwise not to face them squarely while time remains. . . . I do not believe that Soviet Russia desires war. What they desire is the fruits of war and the indefinite expansion of their power and doctrines.

— Document 25 —

W. G. SUMNER: *REPLY TO A SOCIALIST*, 1904 [39]

Combining Herbert Spencer's social Darwinism with Adam Smith's laisser-faire liberalism, W. G. Sumner became the most influential philosophical spokesman for big business, "rugged individualism," and the Old Guard wing of the Republican party. Laisser-faire and commercialism are deemed anti-conservative by most philosophical conservatives; see Coleridge, Carlyle, Disraeli (chapters 5 and 6) on organic vs. atomistic society. Yet a document ably representing the commercialists, whether or not one must call them pseudo-conservative, also merits inclusion in order fairly to cover all major variations. And this Sumner document does indeed share two key points with more genuine conservatives: defense of property, distrust of abstract socialist utopias.

↑   ↑   ↑

. . . The notion that everybody ought to be happy, and equally happy with all the rest, is the fine flower of the philosophy which has been winning popularity for two hundred years. All the petty demands of natural rights, liberty, equality, etc., are only stepping-stones toward this philosophy, which is really what is wanted. All through human history some have had good fortune and some ill fortune. . . . When we talk of "changing the system," we ought to understand that that means abolishing luck and all the ills of life. We might as well talk of abolishing storms, excessive heat and cold, tornadoes, pestilences, diseases, and other ills. Poverty belongs to the struggle for existence, and we are all born into that struggle. . . .

Neither is there any practical sense or tangible project behind the suggestion to redistribute property. . . . A redistribution of property means universal war. The final collapse of the French Revolution was due to the proposition to redistribute property. Property is the opposite of poverty; it is our bulwark against want and distress, but also against disease and all other ills, which, if it can not prevent them, it still holds at a distance. If we weaken the security of property or deprive people of it, we plunge into distress those who now are above it.

Property is the condition of civilization. It is just as

[39] W. G. Sumner, *Selected Essays,* edited by R. R. Davie, New Haven, 1924; the above chapter rebuts Upton Sinclair's article, "The Socialist Party," *Collier's,* October 29, 1904.

essential to the state, to religion, and to education as it is to food and clothing. In the form of capital it is essential to industry, but if capital were not property it would not do its work in industry. If we negative or destroy property we arrest the whole life of civilized society and put men back on the level of beasts. The family depends on property; the two institutions have been correlative throughout the history of civilization. Property is the first interest of man in time and in importance. We can conceive of no time when property was not, and we can conceive of no social growth in which property was not the prime condition. The property interests is also the one which moves all men, including the socialists, more quickly and deeply than any other. Property is that feature of the existing "industrial system" which would most stubbornly resist change if it was threatened in its essential character and meaning. There is a disposition now to apologize for property, even while resisting attack upon it. This is wrong. Property ought to be defended on account of its reality and importance, and on account of its rank among the interests of men.

— Document 26 —

MAURICE BARRÈS: *THE UNDYING SPIRIT OF FRANCE,* 1916[40]

Here is the mystical extreme of that nationalist conservatism which replaced, by what in Part One was defined as "the great reversal," the internationalist conservatism of Metternich, q.v.

✓   ✓   ✓

. . . France was when no such thing existed as Germanic consciousness, or Italian or English consciousness;

[40] Maurice Barrès, *The Undying Spirit of France,* trans. by Margaret Corwin, New Haven, 1917; note especially pp. 2, 4, 19, 23-58. French original: *Les traits éternels de la France,* Paris, 1916. Reprinted by permission of Yale University Press.

in truth we were the first nation of all Europe to grasp the idea of constituting a home-land . . . ever hearkening the call to a crusade and needing, as it were, but the voice from a supernatural world to bring forth . . . heroism. And what does the war [*World War I*] make of these youths and old men? A brotherhood. . . . The soil of the trenches is holy ground; it is saturated with blood, it is saturated with spirituality.

This intimate brotherhood, this community of spirit, continuing throughout two years of warfare, results in giving to certain military units a collective soul. Certain among these souls are characterized by such nobility, sending forth a radiance comparable to that of the Saints, that other groups receive an increment to their own spirit. . . . For more than a thousand years now, this mighty stream of feats of valor has been flowing in undiminished volume. . . . The French make war as a religious duty. They were the first to formulate the idea of a holy war. . . . The mothers understand and share this sacred enthusiasm. . . . A gardener at Lourdes, sorely wounded, died at the hospital; . . . his wife said simply: "He died for his country, she was his mother, I am only his wife. . . ." It would seem, indeed, that we have known only the chrysalis form and that an entire people is unfolding its wings. . . . A woman of the common people receives notification of the death of her husband on the field of honor while she is holding in her arms her babe to whom she is giving nourishment. She reels, straightens up again and cries: *"Vive la France,"* holding up her son toward Heaven. Child of martyrs, offspring of thirty generations of such, thou shalt live tomorrow in a victorious France.

— Document 27 —

IRVING BABBITT: *DEMOCRACY AND LEADERSHIP,* 1924 [41]

[41] Irving Babbitt, *Democracy and Leadership,* Boston, Houghton, Mifflin, 1924, pp. 243-247. Reprinted by permission.

A clear definition of direct vs. indirect democracy.

↗   ↗   ↗

The American reading his Sunday paper in a state of lazy collapse is perhaps the most perfect symbol of the triumph of quantity over quality that the world has yet seen. Whole forests are being ground into pulp daily to minister to our triviality. One is inclined, indeed, to ask, in certain moods, whether the net result of the movement that has been sweeping the Occident for several generations may not be a huge mass of standardized mediocrity. . . . We have already been reminded by certain developments in this country of Byron's definition of democracy as an "aristocracy of blackguards. . . ."

The opposition between traditional standards and an equalitarian democracy based on the supposed rights of man has played an important part in our own political history, and has meant practically the opposition between two types of leadership. . . . America stood from the start for two different views of government that have their origin in different views of liberty and ultimately of human nature. The view that is set forth in the Declaration of Independence assumes that man has certain abstract rights; it has, therefore, important points of contact with the French revolutionary "idealism." The view that inspired our Constitution, on the other hand, has much in common with that of Burke. If the first of these political philosophies is properly associated with Jefferson, the second has its most distinguished representative in Washington. The Jeffersonian liberal has faith in the goodness of the natural man, and so tends to overlook the need of a veto power . . . embodied in institutions that should set bounds to its ordinary self as expressed by the popular will at any particular moment. The contrast that I am establishing is, of course, that between a constitutional and a direct democracy. There is an opposition of first principles between those who maintain that the popular will should prevail, but only after it has been purified of what is merely impulsive and ephemeral, and those who maintain that this will should prevail immediately and unrestrictedly. The American experiment in democracy has, therefore, from the outset been ambiguous, and will remain so until the irrepressible conflict between a Washingtonian and a Jeffersonian liberty has been fought to a conclusion.

— Document 28 —

ORTEGA y GASSET: *THE REVOLT OF THE MASSES, 1930*[42]

Although Ortega's concept of the massman was expressed earlier and more originally in the documents (q.v.) from Burckhardt and Nietzsche, no other book has made so influential and dramatic an impact in warning the world against modern mass barbarism. Here is a conservative warning from an aristocratic Spanish liberal.

✦　　　✦　　　✦

. . . Heap after heap of human beings have been dumped on to the historic scene at such an accelerated rate that it has been difficult to saturate them with traditional culture. . . . What is he like, this mass-man who today dominates public life, political and non-political, and why? . . . Nothing is happening now which was not foreseen a hundred years ago. "The masses are advancing," said Hegel in apocalyptic fashion. "Without some new spiritual influence, our age, which is a revolutionary age, will produce a catastrophe," was the pronouncement of Comte. "I see the flood-tide of nihilism rising," shrieked Nietzsche from a crag of the Engadine. . . . The nineteenth century was of its essence revolutionary. This aspect is not to be looked for in the scenes of the barricades, which are mere incidents, but in the fact that it placed the average man—the great social mass—in conditions of life radically opposed to those by which he had always been surrounded. It turned his public existence upside down. Revolution is not the uprising against pre-existing order, but the setting up of a new order contradictory to the traditional one. . . .

[42] José Ortega y Gasset, *The Revolt of the Masses,* New York, 1932, pp. 55-57, 59-63, 79-82. The Spanish original, *La Rebelión de las Masas,* was published in 1930. Reprinted by permission of W. W. Norton & Co., Inc.

The world which surrounds the new man from his birth does not compel him to limit himself in any fashion, it sets up no veto in opposition to him; on the contrary, it incites his appetite, which in principle can increase indefinitely. . . . There are few men who doubt that motor-cars will in five years' time be more comfortable and cheaper than today. They believe in this as they believe that the sun will rise in the morning. The metaphor is an exact one. For, in fact, the common man, finding himself in a world so excellent, technically and socially, believes that it has been produced by nature, and never thinks of the personal efforts of highly-endowed individuals which the creation of this world presupposed. Still less will he admit the notion that all these facilities still require the support of certain difficult human virtues, the least failure of which would cause the rapid disappearance of the whole magnificent edifice. . . .

Under the species of Syndicalism and Fascism there appears for the first time in Europe a type of man who does not want to give reasons or to be right but simply shows himself resolved to impose his opinions. . . . Here I see the most palpable manifestation of the new mentality of the masses, due to their having decided to rule society without the capacity for doing so. . . . Hence, the "new thing" in Europe is to "have done with discussions"; and detestation is expressed for all forms of intercommunion which imply acceptance of objective standards, ranging from conversation to Parliament, and taking in science. This means a renunciation of the common life based on culture, which is subject to standards, and a return to the common life of barbarism. All the normal processes are suppressed in order to arrive directly at the imposition of what is desired. . . .

Civilization is nothing else than the attempt to reduce force to being the last resort. . . . "Direct action" consists in inverting the order and proclaiming violence as the first resort, or strictly as the sole resort. It is the norm which proposes the annulment of all norms. . . . It is the Magna Charta of barbarism.

— Document 29 —

GEORGE SANTAYANA: *DOMINA-TIONS AND POWERS*, 1951 [43]

The urbane Spanish-American philosopher here alleges
that liberalism is finished, owing to an inherent contradic-
tion between its peaceful tolerance and its unpeaceful
yen to reform the world.

✓ ✓ ✓

. . . The hope of a profound peace was one of the
chief motives in the liberal movement. The traditional
order, which was pregnant with all sorts of wars, civil,
foreign, religious, and domestic, was to be relaxed precisely for the sake of peace. . . . When we have con-
ceded everything that anybody clamors for, everyone
will be satisfied. . . . Swimming in the holiday pond of
a universal tolerance, we may confidently call our souls
our own. . . . So, all grievances being righted and everyone quite free, we hoped in the nineteenth century to
remain for ever in unchallengeable enjoyment of our
private property, our private religions, and our private
morals.

But there was a canker in this rose. The dearest friend
and ally of the liberal was the reformer; perhaps even
his own inmost self was a prepotent Will, not by any
means content with being let alone, but aspiring to
dominate everything. Why were all those traditional con-
straints so irksome? Why were all those old ideas so
ridiculous? Because I had a Will of my own to satisfy
and an opinion of my own to proclaim. Relaxing the
order of society, so as to allow me to live, is by no
means enough, if the old absurdities and the old institutions continue to flourish. . . . No pond is large enough
for this celestial swan . . . no scurry into backwaters
will save the ducks and geese from annihilation. How
should I live safe or happy in the midst of such creatures? . . . [*Hence*] the price of peace, as men are

[43] George Santayana, *Dominations and Powers*, New York,
1951, pp. 447-449. Reprinted by permission of Scribner's.

actually constituted, is the suppression of almost all their liberties. The history of liberalism, now virtually closed, illustrates this paradox.

— Document 30 —

FRANK TANNENBAUM: *A PHILOS-OPHY OF LABOR*, 1952[44]

Contrast this defense of trade-unions as "the great conservative counter-revolution" against liberal and capitalist laisser-faire *with Sumner's conservative defense of that same* laisser-faire, *to which equal space has here been given* (Document 25).

✓   ✓   ✓

Trade-unionism is the conservative movement of our time. It is the counter-revolution. Unwittingly, it has turned its back upon most of the political and economic ideas that have nourished western Europe and the United States during the last two centuries. In practice, though not in words, it denies the heritage that stems from the French Revolution and from English liberalism. It is also a complete repudiation of Marxism. This profound challenge to our time has gone largely unnoticed because the trade-union's preoccupation with the detailed frictions that flow from the worker's relation to his job seemed to involve no broad program. In tinkering with the little things—hours, wages, shop conditions, and security in the job—the trade-union is, however, rebuilding our industrial society upon a different basis from that envisioned by the philosophers, economists, and social revolutionaries of the eighteenth and nineteenth centuries.

In contrast with [*communism, fascism, and* laisser-faire *capitalism*] the trade-union has involved a clustering of men about their work. This fusion [*the new, medieval-style organic society*] has been going on for a long time. It has been largely unplanned. . . . But its very lack

[44] Frank Tannenbaum, *A Philosophy of Labor*, New York, 1952, pp. 3-5, 76, 77, 78, 198-199. Reprinted by permission of Alfred A. Knopf, Inc.

of ideas made it strong. . . . It has gathered power within the community until it has suddenly dawned upon men that a new force—not an idea, but a new force—has come into being. . . . There is a great tradition of humanism and compassion in European and American politics, philosophy, and law, which counters, at first ineffectively, the driving forces operating for the atomization of society and the isolation of man. That tradition in England includes such names as Cobbett, Shaftesbury, Romilly, Dickens, Byron, Coleridge, Carlyle, Ruskin, Charles Kingsley, and many others. It also includes popular movements, such as Christian Socialism, friendly societies, consumers' co-operatives, mechanics' schools, Sunday schools, and Methodist chapels. . . . The trade-union is the real alternative to the authoritarian state. The trade-union is our modern "society," the only true society that industrialism has fostered. As a true society it is concerned with the whole man, and embodies the possibilities of both the freedom and the security essential to human dignity.

— Document 31 —

WALL STREET JOURNAL, A PROUD NAME, 1955 [45]

Our little introductory survey has throughout avoided those neat oversimplifications of definition which would have been more convenient but more misleading. As the present document says, "conservatism defies definition," being no mere "political slogan" but a complex mixture between politics, temperament, ethics, and even aesthetics. In concluding our survey, it may be noted that this complexity is illustrated by the following fact: conservatism is claimed not only by the Wall Street Journal, *that able defender of big-city industrialists, but also by an able trade-union spokesman* (Document 30) *and by able anti-industrialist defenders of rural aristocracy like Coleridge* (Document 6).

[45] Editorial in *Wall Street Journal*, New York, April 29, 1955.

✓   ✓   ✓

Inquiring reporters scurry about the country and note in wonder "the new conservative trend." . . . This public attention to the conservative philosophy is something new for our day. . . . But . . . the feeling for the values of conservatism has been abiding in the people all along. . . . In large part it was hidden by the cloak of language. Very vocal men equated it with "turning back the clock" to McKinley's times, which no one wants to do any more. . . . So did our own Revolution long disguise the fact that it was wrought by men with a deep sense of conservatism. . . . And finally, we think, it was hidden by the fact that conservatism defies definition. . . . Unlike the brave new worlds and the promises of paradise, it cannot be coined into a political slogan.

For conservatism is not a policy; nor is it a program to solve economic or political problems. It is hardly more than an instinctive belief that today's society is built on several thousand years and that in those years men have found things they should fasten to. Out of this grows not opposition to a change in political institutions or in economic methods but an awareness that in too hasty flight from the old we can flee to evils we know not of. . . . The instinct to conserve, we think, never left the American people.

BIBLIOGRAPHICAL NOTE:
SUGGESTED READINGS
FOR STUDENTS

The following documents are so important to conservative thought that they should be read in full by any student here stimulated to specialize in the subject: Burke's *Reflections,* the *Federalist* papers of Hamilton, Madison, and Jay, the *Selected Writings* of John and John Quincy Adams, Coleridge's *On the Constitution of the Church and State,* Calhoun's *Disquisition* and *Discourse,* Cortés's *Essay on Catholicism, Authority, and Order,* the selected speeches of British Tories (Disraeli etc.) in R. J. White's *The Conservative Tradition,* Tocqueville's *Democracy in America* and *Reflections,* Pobiedonostsev's *Reflections of a Russian Statesman,* Sir Henry Maine's *Popular Government,* Irving Babbitt's *Democracy and Leadership,* the memoirs of Metternich and those of Churchill (both too voluminous for most students but important to browse in), and Maistre's *Soirées de Saint Petersbourg.* These books are available in most American college libraries. Excerpts from each appear in Part II, where the reader will find in the footnotes the full details needed in regard to edition, date, place.

Readers interested in more recent developments may consult the books of America's "New Conservatives." These younger scholars and other contemporary American Burkeans are listed on page 107. The author is less familiar with the names of current British intellectual exponents of conservatism; but any list would include David Clarke, Christopher Dawson, William Deakin, Keith Feiling, Quinton Hogg, Christopher Hollis, Douglas Jerrold, Malcolm Muggeridge, Michael Oakeshott, T. E. Utley, F. A. Voigt, R. J. White. The author's other books on conservatism (P. Viereck, *Conservatism Revisited,* 1949; *Shame and Glory of the Intellectuals,* 1952; *The Unadjusted Man,* 1956) contain the qualifications and elaborations omitted from this deliberately-brief introductory survey of a philosophy ever fascinating, ever elusive.

Index of Persons[1]

[1] Persons only (including their adjectives: e.g. "Burkean" indexed under "Burke"). Main subjects, main books are listed in the detailed tables of contents and documents. Titled names are not indexed under "de", "von"; e.g. "D'Alembert" under "A".

VAN NOSTRAND ANVIL BOOKS already published

1 *MAKING OF MODERN FRENCH MIND*—Kohn
2 *THE AMERICAN REVOLUTION*—Morris
3 *THE LATE VICTORIANS*—Ausubel
4 *WORLD IN THE 20th CENTURY*—Rev. Ed. Snyder
5 *50 DOCUMENTS OF THE 20th CENTURY*—Snyder
6 *THE AGE OF REASON*—Snyder
7 *MARX AND THE MARXISTS*—Hook
8 *NATIONALISM*—Kohn
9 *MODERN JAPAN*—Rev. Ed. Tiedemann
10 *50 DOCUMENTS OF THE 19th CENTURY*—Snyder
11 *CONSERVATISM*—Viereck
12 *THE PAPACY*—Corbett
13 *AGE OF THE REFORMATION*—Bainton
14 *DOCUMENTS IN AMERICAN HISTORY*—Morris
15 *CONTEMPORARY AFRICA*—Rev. Ed. Wallbank
16 *THE RUSSIAN REVOLUTIONS OF 1917*—Curtiss
17 *THE GREEK MIND*—Agard
18 *BRITISH CONSTITUTIONAL HISTORY SINCE 1832*—Schuyler and Weston
19 *THE NEGRO IN THE U.S.*—Logan
20 *AMERICAN CAPITALISM*—Hacker
21 *LIBERALISM*—Schapiro
22 *THE FRENCH REVOLUTION, 1789-1799*—Gershoy
23 *HISTORY OF MODERN GERMANY*—Snyder
24 *HISTORY OF MODERN RUSSIA*—Kohn
25 *NORTH ATLANTIC CIVILIZATION*—Kraus
26 *NATO*—Salvadori
27 *DOCUMENTS IN U.S. FOREIGN POLICY*—Brockway
28 *AMERICAN FARMERS' MOVEMENTS*—Shannon
29 *HISTORIC DECISIONS OF SUPREME COURT*—Swisher
30 *MEDIEVAL TOWN*—Mundy and Riesenberg
31 *REVOLUTION AND REACTION 1848-1852*—Bruun
32 *SOUTHEAST ASIA AND WORLD TODAY*—Buss
33 *HISTORIC DOCUMENTS OF W. W. I*—Snyder
34 *HISTORIC DOCUMENTS OF W. W. II*—Langsam
35 *ROMAN MIND AT WORK*—MacKendrick
36 *SHORT HISTORY OF CANADA*—Masters
37 *WESTWARD MOVEMENT IN U.S.*—Billington
38 *DOCUMENTS IN MEDIEVAL HISTORY*—Downs
39 *HISTORY OF AMERICAN BUSINESS*—Cochran
40 *DOCUMENTS IN CANADIAN HISTORY*—Talman
41 *FOUNDATIONS OF ISRAEL*—Janowsky
42 *MODERN CHINA*—Rowe
43 *BASIC HISTORY OF OLD SOUTH*—Stephenson
44 *THE BENELUX COUNTRIES*—Eyck
45 *MEXICO AND THE CARIBBEAN*—Hanke
46 *SOUTH AMERICA*—Hanke
47 *SOVIET FOREIGN POLICY, 1917-1941*—Kennan
48 *THE ERA OF REFORM, 1830-1860*—Commager
49 *EARLY CHRISTIANITY*—Bainton
50 *RISE AND FALL OF THE ROMANOVS*—Mazour
51 *CARDINAL DOCUMENTS IN BRITISH HISTORY*—Schuyler and Weston
52 *HABSBURG EMPIRE 1804-1918*—Kohn
53 *CAVOUR AND UNIFICATION OF ITALY*—Salvadori
54 *ERA OF CHARLEMAGNE*—Easton and Wieruszowski
55 *MAJOR DOCUMENTS IN AMERICAN ECONOMIC HISTORY, Vol. I*—Hacker
56 *MAJOR DOCUMENTS IN AMERICAN ECONOMIC HISTORY, Vol. II*—Hacker
57 *HISTORY OF THE CONFEDERACY*—Vandiver
58 *COLD WAR DIPLOMACY*—Graebner
59 *MOVEMENTS OF SOCIAL DISSENT IN MODERN EUROPE*—Schapiro
60 *MEDIEVAL COMMERCE*—Adelson
61 *THE PEOPLE'S REPUBLIC OF CHINA*—Buss
62 *WORLD COMMUNISM*—Hook
63 *ISLAM AND THE WEST*—Hitti